Savour of the Soul

Divine blessings from
Acharya Vijay Ramchandrasuriswarji Maharajsaheb

Sadhvi Ramya Darshana Shriji

Become Shakespeare.com

First published in 2016 by
BecomeShakespeare.com

Wordit Content Design & Editing Services Pvt Ltd
Newbridge Business Centre, C38/39,
Parinee Crescenzo Building, G Block,
Bandra Kurla Complex, Bandra East,
Mumbai 400 051, India T: +91 8080226699

Copyright © 2016

All rights reserved. Any unauthorized reprint or use of this material is prohibited. No part of this book may be reproduced or transmitted in any form or by any means, electronic or mechanical, including photocopying, recording, or by any information storage and retrieval system without express written permission from the author/publisher.
Please do not participate in or encourage piracy of copyrighted materials in violation of the author's rights. Purchase only authorized editions.

ISBN: 978-93-52017-33-1

CREDITS

Editor: Smt. Neelam Momaya

Publisher Partner: Smt. Sonal Chetan Mehta

Email: devanshu.gemini@gmail.com

Designed and Printed by - Wordit CDE

Available at:

Shailesh C. Kothari
B/10, Jineshwar Darshan, Navroji Lane, Ghatkopar West,
Mumbai 400086
Phone No: +919320105001

Sonal C. Mehta
57, Panorama, 5th Floor, 203, Teen Batti, Opp Dena Bank,
Walkeshwar, Mumbai 40006
Phone No: +919029021361

Rita Girish Jogani
11/2, Dasha Parwad Society,
Behind Paldi Bus Stand, Ahmedabad
Phone No: +919428356884

NaginBhai C. Sheth
504, Jay Tower, Behind Bldg 25,
Govindnagar, Sodawala Lane,
Borivali West

Jayshree Mayur Shah
6, Jamnadas Mansion,
Laxminarayan Lane, Matunga East,
Phone No: +9920067533

Sponsored By:

Smt. Sangeeta Mukesh Mehta

Shri Shailesh Chandulal Kothari

Shri Milan Sheth

Shri Jayesh Kuwadia

PREFACE

In this metaphysical world, books give a soul to the universe, wings to the mind, flight to the imagination and life to everything.

This book by Respected Ramyadarshana Shreeji Maharajsaheb is a superb line-

- From the physical world to the metaphysical world
- From the world of the body into the realm of the soul
- From the abode of suffering into the world of eternal joy
- From the mortal world to the immortal world

It is a bridge joining the two banks taking the soul from its bodily state to its bodiless liberated blissful form...

It is a transformation from the form to the formless

- From bondage to freedom
- From sorrow to unending joy
- From pain to ultimate bliss

Resp. Maharajsaheb has beautifully and aesthetically handled all the stages of the body and compared it to its counterparts on the soul. Eventually, she takes us from the mortal perishable body to the eternal and imperishable joyous world of *"Moksh"*, the ultimate salvation. The miraculous world, the entry into which gives one freedom from the vicious circle of births and deaths... from anguish... from sadness... from pain of separation...from longing... from craving from wants... in short from the bad temporal world to the ecstatic world of infinite glee, cheerfulness, euphoria, joy, jubilation, vivacity, beatitude, ecstasy... to the *Moksh*.

Sr. NO	The Physical World Body	Metaphysical Soul
1	The positive phase of the body – good health	The positive phase of the soul – peace of mind, happiness
2	The disturbing tormenting phase – ill health, disease, infections	The disturbing phase of the soul – *karma*, vices, infection.
3	The unawareness of the troubling phase – known by its symptoms	The unawareness of troubling phase – known by the prominent symptoms
4	The cure from this upheaval phase – the doctor – the physician	The cure from the upheavals – guru (mentor) -> true preceptor ->*sadguru* -> seer
5	Types of disturbance - Mental illness, physical inabilities, diseases, ill functioning organs, old age pain. Diseases like arthritis, schizophrenia makes our body unfit for *Aradhna*	Symptoms that torment the soul: - 1. Anger 2. Greed 3. Attachment 4. Deceit 5. Violence 6. Ego 7. Lie 8. Unchastely 9. Stealing 10. Possession 11. Sorrow 12. Fear 13. anxiety
6	Which living beings are not apt to procure healthy stage- the ones who live in slums, etc.	Which souls are not apt to procure healthy stage- 83 lakh nuclei
7	Competent living beings those are apt to procure healthy stage- the ones who live in a healthy domain.	Competent souls for procuring healthy stage- human soul.

8	The remedy: Internal medicines, external applications and abstinence from things that aggravate the disease.	The remedy- the various aspects of dharma – 1. *Dana* – charity 2. Celibacy – *brahmacharya* (Abstinence from sex) 3. Tap – penance 4. Auspicious inclination-*bhav*
9	The after effects of the remedy – cure, partial cure and improvement in health	The after effects of remedy: The realization of our faults, vices Inclination to redeem the disease Abstain from the vices as far as possible Change in life Leniency in the end of vices Partial restrain Self control, refraining from acts of vices Moderation of indulgence The practice of the opposite virtues like: *Samata* against *raag* Forgiveness against anger, Rage *Nisparigrah* against possession *Abrahmacharya* against *brahmacharya* Truth versus asatya In short treating short comings with the corresponding virtues

10	The visible change-an energetic body	The visible change-an exuberant cheerful soul
11	The lucky ones: Those who have procured treatment and those who follow the line of medicine given to them.	The Lucky ones: those who admit their vices, those who continue in their path of improvement by following the vein of treatment given by their *sadguru*
12	The fortunate ones: The cured people. The people who realize that all this suffering is going to continue in the temporal world and shift to the land of penances-the soul land	The fortunate ones: The enunciated souls, the ascetic souls, the *sadhus* and *sadhvis* and the souls who realize that joy is not in indulgence but in renunciation, in short the liberated souls.

ACKNOWLEDGEMENT

I pay deep reverence and express heartfelt gratitude to my spiritual father, my beloved guru Acharya Ramchandrasuriswarji Maharajsaheb to reveal this notion in me.

My heartfelt thanks to all my philosophers and well-wishers who guided me and walked that extra mile with me to make my dream of a stroll come true. I would also like to express my deep gratitude to:

Gacchadipati Acharya Vijay Punyapal Suriswarji M.S. for laying his trust on me, and also to Acharya Vijay Kritiyash Suriswarji M.S. for guiding me.

I am thankful to Muni Samvegyash Vijay M.S. for spurring me to present this book for the current generation, a move that will help them prosper in this birth and in the next too.

I bow to my Guru Sadhviji Chandrana Shriji M.S.

I am deeply obliged to Sadhviji Nandiswara Shriji, Charudarshana Shriji and Benmaharaj Taporatna Shriji M.S. for giving me space and leisure to complete this task.

I am also indebted to Shobhanaben, my Sansari mother, the one who has installed these values in me, chiseled and honed my life stone from the very onset, and moulded me into a personified sculpture.

I would also like to express my gratitude to Shravika Neelam Dalesh Momaya and Devanshu Shailesh Kothari who have helped to portray my ideas beautifully and aided me in editing the manuscript at each and every phase.

INDEX

1. The Heart of Happiness — 13
2. Moksh — 19
3. Karma — 27
4. Raga — 68
5. Anger — 77
6. Ego — 80
7. Deceit — 84
8. Avarice — 88
9. Envy — 93
10. Brahmacharya and Abrahmacharya — 99
11. Sadguru — 104
12. Knowledge of Birth Spheres — 111
13. The Essence of Human Birth — 115
14. Dharma — 123
15. Forgiveness — 129
16. Micchami Dukkddam — 134
17. Introspection — 139
18. Gratitude — 146
19. Attitude — 149
20. Diksha — 154
21. Shravak and Shravika Dharma — 161
22. Reading-The Stimulus for the Soul — 182
23. Samyak Gyan — 186
    Glossary — 194

Chapter 1

THE HEART OF HAPPINESS
THE INNATE NATURE OF THE SOUL

TRUE HAPPINESS/DELUSIVE HAPPINESS

All human beings focus inherently towards mirth and serene happiness but few realize the significance of true joy, true happiness and the factors that build up this mirth. Today, mirth or happiness is associated with 'accumulating wealth', amassing millions and billions; but when we ponder over it, this is a mirage and history has many evidences showing that money is not a criteria for happiness.

John D Rockefeller was one such multi-millionaire for whom money could not buy happiness. His biography tells us that by the age of 50, his life was a wreck. He was the wealthiest man in the world, yet he was very miserable. He was sick-physically, mentally, emotionally and spiritually and all his million dollars could not award him glee and could not give him pleasure.

He turned into a new leaf and stopped adding to his wealth. He began to distribute away his wealth. Thus was born the Rockefeller Foundation. John Rockefeller rewrote and redefined the meaning of elation for himself. This is the essence of life; to make the best use for the needy and suffering, to give alms and to indulge in charitable acts is one of the virtues of the soul. Mere amassment of wealth and possessions and developing attachment towards them is a vice, as it slowly paves way to greed.

So the equation is: Virtue=Bliss & Peace
Vices=suffering and agony

The second illusion is that people equate 'happiness' with 'power and position'

A fond mother proudly declared that her son had acquired happiness at the early age of 23. He had been appointed as the managing director of a large industrial concern but as he would have it, his success went into his head and he started behaving rudely with his colleagues. He became unpopular with his workers and remained sullen. He developed a bad temper and fell victim to two big vices- gambling and drinking. What did his power and positions award him with? The mainspring of low inhabitant in long term and in short term, it results in loss of power, position and peace.

When one cannot digest the newly acquired power and position, it tarnishes his ego, with the result that the loss of power leads to loss of discrimination power of the mind and in turn encourages sabotage habits, addictions. The evil and disastrous results of which are carried not only in this birth but in the successive births as well, it thereby affects numerous incarnations too.

Should then the people with power and high position be put in the category of beatitude?

The third illusion is that many of us equate ecstasy with visible mundane materialistic acquisition; there are numerous illustrations in life for this illusion. There are many women who wear expensive attires and adorn their physique cup-a-pie with ornaments, their bags filled with hard cash. They ride about in Mercedes and Sedan. Onlookers would certainly agree that they have reached the highest scale of happiness in life, as power, position and the material abundance is clearly visible.

But now, see the climax, the reality show. When the woman was asked if she was happy, she broke down and admitted sadly, "I am the unhappiest woman in this world; my husband is constantly running after other women. He is not interested in me anymore and does not pay any attention to me."

Would we call this woman happy? Is she in glee in spite of all the power, all the riches, all the possessions?

Which would otherwise make other woman jealous? How can then these be equated with happiness? Have we ever pondered?

The fourth illusion... *Raga*...

The devices of happiness have taken in its clinch the whole mundane world. **'Raga'** or **'attachment'** for mundane objects and worldly persons is the root cause of all the pain, agony, all suffering; it is the mother of hatred of all vices. It becomes perceptible as suffering for the soul. Hatred in itself is a lucid feeling which perturbs the soul and *raga* is the sugar coated emotion which stirs and disturbs the soul. In the case of the unhappy woman, her attachment towards her husband made her disturbed and unhappy and these feelings found vent in her hatred towards all the other women her husband ran after.

So, what is the definition of happiness? What is true happiness? Evidence and proof are proving the fact that opulence, wealth, position, power, status, love, affection and mundane objects are not devices or sources for procuring real happiness but inner virtues, true knowledge, magnanimity of mind, and bona fide character are the ladders leading to the supreme splendid savory phase of the souls and in the consequent serenity of the soul.

As is rightly said:

If wealth is lost, something is lost

If health is lost, much is lost

If peace (of soul and body) is lost, then everything is lost.

The outer worldly things touch only the fringes of life. They are not able to penetrate into the depths of life.

A man, who has all worldly riches, may be intellectually barren. He may be emotionally unbalanced, frustrated and spiritually sterile. The secret behind happiness is the controlling and understanding of our emotions. If we are able to conquer our emotion and acquire a mastery over them, then we are our own master. If we don't allow any emotion to impasse or step over our peace, then happiness will not elude us. Success can then be truly defined as the ability to be happy, remain happy and make others happy. The sheer spiritual happiness is the natural state of the soul. The ability to love and be loved not in the form of *raga* or attachment, but to develop true beneficent feeling for all living beings is the secret to true happiness. It is the true essence of religion. In Latin, it literally means 'nature'. Religion teaches us to remain in the domain of our true nature. There is no happiness which wealth can buy but you can become wealthy when you discover the true treasure of your virtues, the limitless joy imbibed in the vicinity of the soul, the happiness that result in the true state of the soul is its *"Sahaj Ananddasha"*. The immense joy that comes naturally cannot be bought. It has to be experienced.

HAPPINESS IS OUR DOMINANCE

Happiness is the only monopoly of the soul. It is nature of the soul. It is virtue of the soul.

I understand that my reaction to the problem and my low scales of maturity, causes more pain than the problem itself.

When someone is doing something or is about to do something, in a way I don't want it to be done and I am not able to accept it, I get frustrated. However, when someone is doing something and I am able to accept it, I remain calm.

So, it is not someone or something that cause frustration in me or calmness in me.

This elevates the fact that the person (someone) or object (something) is not the direct cause for our happiness or unhappiness, but the culprit is our own feeling, our own reaction which has been endangered due to the person or object.

So, what happens outside me is just my own reaction or response to it that affects my state of mind.

Similarly, when someone has something that I don't have or someone is able to produce the result that I am not able to produce and I am not able to accept it, it is jealousy and when someone has it and I am able to accept it, it is my inspiration.

So, it is with every emotion. With non-acceptance of hurt, it will cause hatred in me but acceptance of hurt prepares me to pardon.

So, it is not 'something' or 'someone' that make me feel positive or negative but it is my 'acceptance' or 'non – acceptance', which is making me feel positive (calm) or negative (perturbed).

So, the next time when you feel perturbed with a negative emotion, instead of asking who or what is disturbing you, replace resistance with acceptance and the negative emotion will turn into a positive one. As everything around us is not in our hand but the ruling of our mind surely is in our control.

It isn't life but it is the quality of your response to what happens in our life that determines the pacification of our life.

This experience helps us to grow in maturity, so that intellectually, by lifting our self; we are, in turn, lifting our spirit repose.

The core is that if we want to be happy, we have to restrain our emotions. It is a remedy for ease and bliss.

Our experience gives horizons to us.

All of us are bound by our instincts, which is to avoid pain and embrace pleasure. For that, think positively and not destructively. Build a constitution of right and wrong and expect man to abide by it.

The power of fortitude and power of choice is a man's greatest boon, which is called an intelligent living. This is great power bestowed on to human beings. With great power comes great responsibility. This is universal law that what favorable or unfavorable things turn up in our life is our own designed *kismat* of past.

There are very lucid examples for that:

We get perturbed if sugar is less in the tea. It's, after all, one teaspoon of sugar and we allow that to disturb our peace and bliss as well as the peace of the surrounding. In monetary terms, one spoon of sugar costs how much? 50 paisa! And you are a *'crorepati'*. Fifty paisa should not disturb a millionaire and spoil the mood of his loved ones. Happily drinking tea without complaining will mean a lot to your peace and your near and dear ones; and still if you don't like the taste of the tea, tell her politely to make another.

Same with the dishes, salt may be slightly more or slightly less in one of the side dishes in your meals and a pinch of salt will be costing how much? So, your peace shouldn't disturb you at all by all these reasons.

This is to be related in all phases of our life.

All the joys of the world are ours for the taking. There is always an end at our disposal. We just need to develop the vision to look at everything with a neutral eye, instead of coloring them up with our prejudices, perception and limited understanding of the situation.

Standing under a *Neem* tree and expecting a mango is futile. So, either change the expectation or change the tree. So, here to change the expectation is in our own hands and by that we can create our peaceful today and in succession tomorrow too.

Chapter 2

MOKSH: THE HEALTHIEST PHASE OF THE SOUL

Moksh means the liberation or the emancipation of the soul from alien matter known as *karma*. It is the most blissful state in the whole existence of the soul.

A liberated soul is a one which has attained its true pristine and original nature - the true self i.e. infinite knowledge, infinite perception and infinite bliss.

Moksh means the sublime rapture of the soul.

- It is a state where there is only pleasure without any pain and suffering.

- It is a state where there is only one desire; the desire to attain complete joyousness, which is possible only in *Moksh*.

- It is the forum which every soul yearns to experience. This is the supreme stage which deals with the height of elation and total sublimity.

- *Moksh* is the perpetual craving for cheerfulness and to move out of the sphere of sorrow, and enter into the land of immortal cheer.

- It is a state of total virtuousness, without even a single fault.

- Materialistic gaiety or happiness is not the true happiness but has a shadow of agony as well. In materialistic pleasure, happiness and unhappiness are stringed together but the concept of *Moksh* is like an antonym to this.

- It is the stage in which all *karma* is dispelled.

- The empire of the *jadh* or *karma* is a mortal world or *sansar* but the soul's empire is *Moksh* - the immortal world!

- The soul's repugnant state is *sansar* and the pleasant state is *Moksh*.

- The fathomless ocean of bliss is what we call *Moksh*.

- The sublime sacred persona of the soul is *Moksh*.

- In this mortal world, we often see a fake and incomplete exuberance. The real, virtual and sheer stage of exuberance is *Moksh*.

- Dependence is the root of all pain and suffering. Independence is the root to all relish. *Moksh* is complete independence from the mortal body and mind. It depicts a free, liberated soul.

- Bondage relates to suffering and freedom from bondage of *karma* is freedom from all pain and suffering. This is called as *Moksh*.

- All precious things come with a cost. Happiness is one of the most coveted luxuries that every one craves for, and if one thinks logically, then it comes absolutely free. It is a precious resource which is dominant in every one's soul. The undermining of this precious resource is *Moksh*.

- *Moksh* is not just a faith. It is a path and metaphysics which can be perceived by perception and self realization in this birth too.

- If one can contemplate, he can perceive that there is not a single object in this mundane world which is apt to confer perpetual and continuous happiness, but *Moksh* on the other hand, has the ability to confer perpetual happiness.

- All actions that we perform in this mortal world are tinted with sins and violence. This *sansar* is colored with the varied hues of sins but the world of *Moksh* is not tinted at all with sins.

- Even the removal of one atom from our sacred soul has the capacity to fill the whole universe with joy; happiness and excitement, so just imagine the capacity of the whole soul. This acquiring of capacity and opening the doors of our very own joyousness is *Moksh*.

- Material happiness available in this world is in reality a phase of unhappiness but *Moksh* is a phase of true and real happiness, a manifestation of vivacity.

- Material happiness is temporary but the happiness of soul is permanent.

- Happiness is an attribute of the soul itself. It emerges from the soul. The body, or as a matter of fact, all non living things do not have the capacity to sense or feel. They cannot experience joy or sorrow as they have no sensation. The sensation is due to the existence of the soul inside. Once the soul leaves, the body is burnt. If it had feelings, would it allow to be tied down and be burnt? No! To settle in one's own quality, is the very nature of every substance in cosmos…

- All souls covet this utter happiness that is offered by *Moksh*.

- The search is universal and unique. From outside, we may be looking for money, possessions, position, name, fame, love and affection but in reality we are trying to experience happiness from these. Some people think accumulating money is the path to happiness, some feel happiness lies in multiplying things of comfort while others associate it with the craze for running after name and fame but some time or the other, in the span of their lives, they realize their folly and understand that happiness cannot be acquired. It comes from within. It is a continuous process which can be eased down by contrasting waves.

Let us analyze the negative and the positive attributes of *Moksh*:

Negative form: There is neither agony or anguish nor any element for agony or anguish.

There is no pain of birth

There is no pain of death

There is no pain of old age

There is no pain of disease

There is no mental pain

There is no physical pain

There is no pain of fear

The positive aspect: There is neither materialistic happiness nor materialistic elements for felicity. The happiness and substances of happiness that are absent in *Moksh* are as follows:

There is an absence of good touch

There is an absence of good smell or the sense of smell

There is an absence of good words

There is an absence of beauty

There is an absence of mind

There is an absence of body itself

In short, there are no sense organs. There is an absence of leisure objects.

Let us try to comprehend the enigma hidden behind the concept of *Moksh* and examine a lucid concept of emancipation.

All worldly souls aspire for happiness. Right? Now what is the media for achieving happiness?

Well, there are two Medias for attaining happiness:

Firstly, the soul depends on material things to acquire happiness. Rather, it uses all non living things or *jadh pudgala* to acquire happiness.

Secondly, the soul uses no outward matter to acquire happiness. It accumulates happiness from its own self.

Now we will endeavor to articulate the first way. The dependence on *jadh padarth* which has its own qualities:

a.) Form- beautiful, ugly, deformed or shapely form

b.) Taste-sour, salty, bitter, sweet

c.) Odour- good smell, bad smell,

d.) Touch-hot, cold, smooth, rough, soft, heavy, light, hard

e.) Each and every atom in this world has these four qualities and all substances in this universe are just different structures of this atom.

The living substance or *atma* acquires happiness through these *jadh* qualities via the province of senses i.e. shape, smell, touch and taste which can differ from time and place. These substances serve as a means of begetting happiness for a short period of time. This is a process of yearning, craving & reaching saturation level and associating it with joy and satisfaction.

For instance, you are hungry and crave food. You get satisfied and associate it with happiness but that is just for a limited period of time, but once you have overeaten, the sight of food can be nauseating. If happiness was in the food, it would have given us joy forever but this is not the case.

Another example is that when you are lustful and develop a physical relation with the opposite sex, you feel content but in truth, psychologists claim that after the culmination, men are left with sadness.

The consequence or aftermath of pleasure is anguish. The universal law claims "what you sow you reap". If we sow pain, we reap pain. Once we start using our five senses as organs of pleasure, we become their slaves. The most important part in this acquiring of sensual pleasures is that it leaves a trail of attachment or *Raga,* and hatred or *dwesh* that acts as the biggest hurdle to the most auspicious virtue of the soul.

The true pristine nature of the soul is tarnished by the violence-*bhavhinsa*– with the consequence, the soul forgets its true nature and indulges in acts of *kashay*–hate and attachment- *Raga* and *Dwesh* and inevitably becomes subdued and suppressed. All its qualities are overshadowed by the clouds of the negative feelings. It remains a prisoner under the influence of these thoughts till he comes in contact with a real seer who shows him the real path and makes him realize his folly and releases him from the clutches of *kashay.* This total freedom is what we call as *Moksh.*

It is true that pleasure and power are compared to honey spread on a sword. It tastes sweet and tempting and when we start relishing it, it cuts our tongue leaving us in pain and suffering. All sensual pleasures are the same.

Now let's proceed to the second path to happiness from the inside. From the true source i.e. our very own soul. From self realization we get to achieve the true meaning of happiness by achieving our true potential. The bright, shining, joyous form of the *'Sahaj Ananddasha* or the form of absolute joyfulness of the soul is exposed.

Take for instance, deep inside the core of the earth there is gold and there are rocks. As long as they stay under the core, there is no difference in their value. Once they are excavated and the gold is revealed, then the value is realized. In the same way, there is no difference in the sleeping potential of all the souls in this universe. But just as the jeweler polishes and creates the true worth of the gold beneath, in the same way our religious guru help us cleanse our impurities and allows the pristine true self to shine. The soul is exposed to its crowning glory, of bliss, tranquility and peace. This is the true picture of *Moksh*.

Moksh can be described as

Meadows of Mirth

Home of Happiness

Bouquet of Beatitude

River of Revel

Beach of Buoyant

Jewels of Joy

Cascade of Chirpiness

Moon of Merriment

Fountain of Felicity

Garden of Glee

Palace of Peace

Grove of Gaiety

Temple of Triumph

Cluster of Cheer

Mountain of merriment

Blossom of Bliss

Emperor of Ecstasy

Monarch of Mirth

Soverign of Savour

It is now necessary for us to make the attainment of *Moksh* as our eminent objective. We should not forget that human birth is apt for this endeavor to acquire right faith, right knowledge and right conduct which are conducive for the attainment of *Moksh*. So, we need to make the maximum use of this opportunity and turn towards our goal.

Chapter 3

KARMA DOCTRINE

The disease phase of the soul

Each and every one of us is bound by the fetters of *Karma*. Our ancient scriptures categorize us as two different types of souls; one is *mukta* and the other is *badha*.

The *muktas* are the liberated or emancipated souls, who through the grace of god and grace of the guru, have succeeded in liberating themselves from the bondage of *Karma*.

The second type- *badhas* are the souls, who are still bound by the toils of their own *Karma*. Many, alas, are still in a state of ignorance about their own condition.

We are now aware of the fetters that bind us! Those, who become aware of their own bonds makes the efforts to seek liberation. In this condition, our deep consciousness is awakened and it urges us on the path of liberation (*i.e. moksh*).

Let's try to dwell on the most profound, wide, deep and complex truths of *Karma* by means of beautiful and simple parables. Every day, the fishermen cast their wide nets into the ocean. A few fishes are caught in the net and many, who have escaped from the net, swim about freely in the ocean *mukta*. But there are a few fishes that are blissfully ignorant and unaware of their condition. They are content to rest positively in the net that ensnares them, unaware of the terrible and painful fate that awaits them, the same is the state of *badha* soul.

Now, the second ones, who are now aware that they are bounded, should not waste their time and energy on futile speculations. They realize the truth that they are bound by their own *Karma* and all their time, energy and effort must be focused on freeing themselves from the bonds of *Karma*!

We have heard the story of a man whose house has caught fire. The neighbours, who rushed out to help him and tried to put out the flames, told him, "Come out of the house or you will soon be reduced to ashes!" The foolish man said to them from within the house that he would not leave this house until they answered three questions of his. "First, who caused the fire? Second, what was the exact temperature of the fire? Third, what are the chemical constituents of the fire? Until I get answers to these three questions, I shall not budge from here."

Incensed by his foolishness and stubbornness, the people asked if this is the time or place to ask such questions. "Get out of this burning inferno and save your life," they yelled, but the man was adamant. "No way," he shouted "I shall not leave this house until my questions have been answered."

Such is the folly of many of us today. We live in the midst of burning flames that threaten to engulf us and we need to make every effort to save ourselves by quenching the leaping flames.

Souls are burning by manifold of *karmic* flames.

Some are trapped in the fire of attachment and hatred, others in the flames of ego and anger and some in flames of greed and deceit, envy and jealousy, some in ignorance, illusion and some in lust, passion. So quench the flames which are the outcome of karmic bonds.

The question that concerns us is what should we do and what can we do to liberate ourselves from the bonds of *Karma*?

Universe is governed by causes and effects, and in turn there are three empirical laws.

Laws that govern cause and effect:

1. If there is an effect, then there must be a cause.
2. Effect is nothing but cause itself in a different form... a different manifestation.
3. If you remove the cause from the effect, then nothing remains.

Example:

1. If there is a gold necklace, then there must be gold. If there is a mud pot, then there must be mud.

2. Isn't the necklace, gold in another form?

   Isn't the mud pot just another form of mud?

   Isn't the effect just another manifestation of the cause?

3. Where is the necklace without the gold? There is no existence of the mud pot without the mud. Where is the question of an effect without the cause?

   Where is the question of an effect (*sansar*) without the cause (*Karma*)?.

   So, to demolish the effect, give up the cause.

   Now, let's dwell on how to demolish *Karma* by procuring knowledge of *Karma*. The perceptible variation and strangeness in this *sansar* is assured evidence for belief of non-perceptible *Karma*.

   When there is perceptible fruit, then it is definitely sure that imperceptible seeds should be there, when there is progeny there is parentage; when there are consequences, there are causes. As there is *sansar* of souls, there is *Karma* Name causes for it.

So, to uproot the dire *sansar*, the acquaintance of *karma* is crucial. Hence, have persistence to acquire acquaintance of *karma*. In this universe, there are eight fold matters (*pudagala*) useful to animate (souls). From these 8 folds, the *karmic* body is one of them. For a layman, *karma* is not a subject of perception but it is subject of conception and inference; which are proof for existence of *karma*.

Onset: First and for most what is trait of *Karma*?

In the universe (*14 Raj-loka- it is the measurement of universe according to Jain doctrine*) the *karmic* matters are being serried. The souls, by various reasons, infuse *karmic* matters with one's own self, after that only karmic matters (*pudgalas*) convert into *Karma* and now it has the power and potentials to impart its effects on soul.

The reasons or causes for influx of *karmic* matters toward souls have four folds:

1. *Mithyatva* : wrong-tenets, wrong conviction.
2. *Avirati*   : non-pledge.
3. *Kashay*   : passion-raga, *dvesh,* anger, conceit, deceit, avarice, etc.
4. *Yoga*   : means to relate via media of mind, speech and physique acts.

1. *Mithyatva cause:* wrong - tenets, wrong conviction

Among these four reason of *Karma bandh,* (*causes of sansar*) the most dreadful reason is first *mithyatva,* (wrong - tenets, wrong conviction) the mother hood of this *sansar*. This reason is being attached to the soul from eternal time. If we want to demolish the *sansar*, we have to demolish the root cause *mithyatva* (perverse vision) from the root. From past so many incarnations, the aspirant souls are doing an attempt to demolish the *sansar* by opposite cause named *dharma* which has potentials to demolish *sansar*. As the trait of *dharma* is to negate the *sansar* and liberate the soul from *karmic* bondage and procure the pinnacle state of happiness, named as *moksh*. But at present, it is perceptible that after performing *dharma* in past many incarnations and present incarnation too; the rotation of soul is intact in *sansar* of 84 Lac species. This proves that there is defect in the cause named *dharma* and if we want the perfect result of *moksh*, the defect from the cause has to be removed and then the factual fruits of *moksh* will be procured by all of us very soon.

Let's try to understand it metaphorically. There is a massive tree, which is standing for decades and is being pervaded in a very huge space, as it is perturbing. It is being removed from the trunk and space is being done neat and clean. But after some days, again, there will be sprouts in that space and the tree will start pervading very fast.

What is the secret behind it? Yes, we will evidently tell that in underground, the roots are yet intact; hence, when surrounding devices are favorable for shoot-up, it begets the tree again, so if we want to uproot the tree for forever, then the tree should be cut off from the roots and not from the trunk.

Similarly, the massive tree of *sansari* soul is standing from eternal time and is being pervaded wide which perturbs the soul by conferring various pains and agonies in 84 Lac species. Hence, the endeavour by aspirant souls to demolish this *sansar* is being done by an agent named *dharma*. It is analogous to removing the tree from the trunk and not from the root. Means *dharma* is being executed but the root of *sansar* named *mithyatva* is intact from past eternal period. Hence, that impure dharma confers the fruits of celestial and human births, but the crux is that the root of *mithyatva* is intact, hence in human and celestial births also, the souls get infatuated in sensual pleasure and passion which results into fetter of *Karma* and that again results into rotation in low inhabitants and consistent births and deaths of the souls in appalling *sansar.*

Hence, a person who has ardent feelings to uproot one's own gruesome *sansar* and wants to procure one's own innate virtues joy named *moksh* should first of all uproot this *mithyatva,* the mother hood of *sansar* (wrong belief, wrong tenets, wrong conviction, and wrong perception) from the soul. Means procuring true beliefs, true tenets, true conviction, true perception, *Samayak Darshan* and *Samyak Gyan* and endeavour for *dharma* which will certainly confer fruits of emancipation to the soul in a short period.

Let's dwell on what is wrong belief *mithyatva?* It is very lucid. It is an illusion that "This venomous *sansar is* being perceived as benevolent *sansar!*'" Venomous *sansar* interprets 'yearn for sensual pleasure and passion'. A snake's venom can halt life for one birth only, but the soul's venomous yearning of sensual pleasure and passion, sails the soul in ocean of infinite births and deaths. What is the crux behind it? What you sow, you shall reap. The base of all sensual pleasures and passions is pain. How come? All sensual pleasures are being received by slaying one to four sense organs. Hence, it is requisite to understand the factual trait of venomous *sansar* and free oneself from clutch of venomous *sansar.*

This also relates to freeing oneself from the clutches of wrong belief means to demolish the illusion, to accede and believe what is the fact.

It has been the axiom in scriptures that for one time also if the strength and capacity of *mithyatva* is broken, then the fruits of its flourishing and the span of *sansar* get limited." Perceive the stupendous importance and purport of sabotaging the strength of *mithyatva* from the soul. There are no words to accolade the significance of sabotaging *Mithyatva* and gain the *Samayak Darshan* (*clarity of vision to gain conviction of the universal truth*) by the soul.

2. Avirati cause: non-pledge

The second reason *Avirati* is being elucidated as absence of any fold of vows in life, *'Virati'* means to accept a vow and 'A' denotes 'no', means no vow - no *virati* means *avirati* in life. Here the clarity of truth is present and wrong tenets are not present, but the soul does not possess strength to desist wrong acts and accept true acts as per the belief, but due to the clarity of vision of *samyak darshan*, the succession of *sansar* is being desisted and in few births, the rotation of soul in *sansar* will eternally halt.

3. Kashay cause, passion- *raga, dvesh,* anger, conceit, deceit, avarice, etc.

The word *Kashay* is made of *'kas'* and *'aya'*. *'Kas'* means *Sansar* and *'aya* means to obtain or gain. Means by doing these strong feelings of *Raga, Dvesh, Krodh, Maan, Maya, Lobh,* etc. is to flourish one's own odious *sansar*. Its outcome is loathsome *sansar*. Its aspects are ahead in *mohaniya Karma*.

4. Yoga cause, relating via media of mind, speech, etc.

Yoga interprets for 'to joint', 'to relate' which means- to relate mind, speech and physique with *ashubh (vile)* deeds. By performing *ashubh* deeds of mind, speech and physique, *ashubh Karma* influxes in the soul and it can be done by own self, by ordering someone to do or by applauding when someone is doing the same.

Among these four reasons, the dense or acute bondage of *Karma* is due to *Mithyatva (wrong-belief)* which begets dreadful and infinite *sansar* of soul, but once the acute *Ras (capacity)* of this *Karma* is partially demolished, then *Moksh* of that soul is certain in short period. To demolish the acute *Ras* of this *Karma* means to do endeavour to gain cent person. Clarity of inner vision means to have conviction that "This venomous *sansar* means penchant for sensual pleasures and passions, undoubtedly its cause is unhappiness, in present also it imparts unhappiness and its outcome too is unhappiness. Hence, when this fact is being carved in the mind and the heart, then the *ras* capacity of *Mithyatva Karma* is being broken which means that the cause of loathsome *sansar* is being uprooted and the result is splendid. The effect of roaming in these gruesome *sansar* is impeded and the illusion due to *Mithyatva* is being deposed.

The sphere of consequence of *Karma* has mainly 3 folds:

1. To confer happiness and material for happiness to every soul in this universe.
2. To confer affliction and material for affliction to every soul in this universe.
3. To suppress the pristine eternal powers of souls and suppress the attributes of souls.

The manifestation of *Karma* has 3 folds.

1. *Bandh (Bondage)*
2. *Uday (effect, consequences of Karma)*
3. *Satta (dormant stage of Karma)*

i. THE FIRST PHASE OF *KARMA: BANDH:-*

By four fold reasons the *Karma* gets fettered with the soul, that phase of soul is known as *Karma Bandh* phase. When the *Karma* gets infused with the soul, four procedures take place in *Karma*, which are:

1. **Prakruti bandh**: *Prakruti* means nature- the specification of quality of *Karma* when it gets bonded on soul is known as *prakruti bandh* of *Karma*.

2. **Sthiti bandh**: *Sthiti* means span- for how much time it will stay *bonded* with the soul is known as *sthiti bandh* of *Karma*.

3. **Rasbandh**: *Ras* means capacity- which is the potential, the capacity of *Karma* to give effect to the soul, densely or sickly, is known as *ras bandh* of *Karma*.

4. **Pradeshbandh**: *Pradesha* means quantity, bondage of quantity of *Karma* on soul is known as *pradesh bandh* of *Karma*.

In these four procedures, the chief is *Rasbandh* and it's the most important. The least important is quantity. This is first phase of *Karma*.

ii. THE SECOND PHASE OF *KARM: UDAY:-*

The *Uday* of *Karma* means the effect phase of *Karma*, ripened phase of *Karma*, outcome or the effect or *uday* of *Karma*. It is always going to be equal to how is the *bandh*. If the *bandh* of *Karma* is good, then the effect is going to be good. E.g. as you sow so shall you reap...

iii. THE THIRD PHASE OF *KARMA: SATTA:-*

The Satta of *Karma* means the stage between *bandh* and *uday*. The passive stage of *Karma*, the ineffective dormant stage of *Karma* i.e. the *Karma* which has been bonded today and it is going to ripen to give effect after 100 days. The period of 1 to 99 days phase of *Karma* is known as *satta* of *Karma*.

The different sorts of *Karma bandh* occur due to different causes. The prime cause of *Karma bandh* is our own inclination and our propensity to do sinful acts. E.g. when there is an inclination to do sinful act but yet the act is not being performed, then also the bond of *Karma* is there and when the sinful act is added, it ignites the inclination. The variation in *Karma bandh* depends on variation in inclination.

For sins (*paap*) *Karma bandh:*

1. The predilection for faults *doshes* results into intense *bandh* of *paap Karma*.

2. The attraction for faults *doshes* results into less intense *bandh* of *paap Karma*.

3. When the faults *doshes* are being performed without attraction, the *bandh* of *paap Karma* is very mild.

Hence, the prudent soul should be aware at the time of bond as the bond stage of *Karma* is in our own control, so to cultivate good or bad *bandh* of *Karma* is in our own hands.

We understood the trait of *Karma* and manifestation of *Karma*, so now we will discuss at length about how many sorts of *Karma* are there and their traits and folds of prime *Karma*.

How Many sorts of *Karma* are there?
There are primarily 8 folds of *Karma*

There are 8 prime folds or attributes of souls. The 8 fold *Karma* suppresses the supreme 8 folds attributes of souls and the sub total of 8 folds of *Karma* has 147 folds.

	Attributes of soul	Suppressing *Karma*
1	*Anantgyan*: infinite knowledge	*Gyan avarniya Karma*
2	*Anant darshan*: infinite perception	*Darshan avarniya Karma*
3	*Anant charitra*: eternal/steadiness	*Mohaniya Karma*
4	*Anantvirya*: infinite energy	*Antaray Karma*
5	*Avyabadha Sukha*: eternal happiness	*Vedniya Karma*
6	*Akshaya sthiti*: immortality	*Aayushya Karma*
7	*Arupitva*: amorphous formless	*Nam Karma*
8	*Aguru laghu*: neither high nor low	*Gotra Karma*

The fold of 8 prime *Karma* are:

1. The sub of *Gyanavarniya Karma* has : 5 folds
2. The sub of *Darshanavarniya Karma* has : 9 folds
3. The sub of *Mohaniya Karma* has : 28 folds
4. The sub of *Antaray Karma* has : 5 folds
5. The sub of *Vedaniya Karma* has : 2 folds
6. The sub of *Aayushya Karma* has : 4 folds
7. The sub of *Nam Karma* has : 93 folds
8. The sub of *Gotra Karma* has : 2 folds
   147 folds

Now we are discussing 8 prime *Karma* and expounding the sub divisions of 8 prime *Karma*.

1. Gyanavarniya Karma: This *Karma* obscures our *gyan* knowledge, by which the knowledge of a person with an omniscient form *kevalgyan* is always covered like an eye with a curtain.

The sub divisions of *Gyanavarniya Karma* has 5 folds:

i. **Matigyanavarniya Karma:** *Mati* means mind. The knowledge *gyan* obtained due to *Mati* mind and 5 senses is known as *matigyan*. The *Karma* which suppresses this *gyan* is known as *matigyanavarniya Karma* which has 28 folds.

ii. **Shrutgyanavarniya Karma:** *Shrut* means *shastra* (scriptures) the knowledge (*gyan*) obtained by the scriptures, written or verbal is known as *shrutgyan*. The *Karma* which suppresses this *gyan* is known as *shrutgyanavarniya* Karma which has 14 folds.

iii. **Avadhigyanavrniya Karma:** The knowledge obtained by soul itself, without devices of mind, senses, and shrut of limited area is called as *Avadhigyan*. *Avadhi* means limit e.g.

knowledge obtained about only *tirchha lok* (*obligue*) place in 14 *raj-lok* is *Avadhigyan* of *tirchha loka*. The *Karma* which suppresses this knowledge completely or partially is known as *avadigyanavarniya Karma*, which has 6 folds.

iv. **Maanhaparyavgyanavarniya Karma:** The knowledge obtained by soul itself without any devices. The knowledge of the *sangni panchendriya* soul thoughts of mind living in *adhidweep* is known as *Maanhaparyavagyan*. *Maanha* means mind, the thought of mind. The *Karma* which suppresses this *gyan* is known as *Maanhaparyavagyanavarniya Karma* which has 2 folds.

v. **Kevalgyanavarniya Karma:** The soul itself obtains knowledge of complete universe (*lok and alok*) of complete substances, place, time, inclination and nature of substances of past, present and future is known as *kevalgyan*, which has no fold.

Keval means only, pure, complete, unique, infinite, unhindered, consistent and sole knowledge. The *Karma* which suppresses this *gyan* of soul is known as *kevalgyanavarniya Karma*.

2. Darshanavarniya Karma: Perception-obscuring *Karma* is the one where someone wishing to see his master is presented by the door-keeper and is not allowed to see him.

It has 9 folds:

	Attributes		Suppressing *Karma*
1.	*Chakshu Darshan*	:	*Chakshudarshanavarniya Karma*
2.	*Achakshu Darshan*	:	*Achakshudarshanavarniya Karma*
3.	*Avadhi Darshan*	:	*Avadhidarshanavarniya Karma*
4.	*Keval Darshan*	:	*Kevaldarshanavarniya Karma*
5.	*Nindra*		
6.	*Nindra Nindra*		

7. Prachala
8. Prachala prachala
9. Thinidhi

i. **Chakshudarshanavarniya Karma**: The perception by eyesight is known as *chakshudarshan*. *Chakshu* means eye sight and *darshan* means perception (*to see*). The knowledge obtained through eye sight is known as *chakshu darshan*. The *Karma* which suppresses this *guna* of soul is known *chakshudarshanavarniya Karma*. The consequence of this *Karma* is rewarded as eye blindness.

ii. **Achakshudarshanavarniya Karma**: The perception via 4 senses leaving eyesight is known as *achakshudarshan*. *Achakshu* means four senses leaving eyesight and *Darshan* means perception. The knowledge obtained through 4 senses i.e. skin, touch, ear and nose is known as *achakshudarshan*. The *Karma* which suppresses this trait (*guna*) of soul is known as *Achakshudarshanavarniya Karma*. The consequence of this *Karma* is: a person can be dumb, speechless stammering, deaf, paralyses, unsound mind, etc.

iii. **Avadhidarshanarvarniya Karma**: In this, the knowledge is directly obtained by the soul without any media of senses and mind. In this Avadhi *darshan*, the perception obtained from 14 *Raj-loka* is of limited place. The *Karma* which suppresses this *guna* of soul is known as *Avadhidarshanavarniya Karma*.

iv. **Kevaldarshanavarniya Karma**: In this too, *darshan* is directly obtained by the soul without any media of senses and mind. In this, the entire universe is being seen by soul which is known as *kevaldarshan* and the *Karma*, which suppresses this guna of soul is known as *kevaldarshan avarniya Karma*.

v. **Nindra**: Means to slumber-the sleep which can be broken by slight efforts. This hinders the perception of complete substance.

vi. **Nindra nindra**: This is deep slumber. This is the type of sleep which can be broken by hard efforts is called *nindra nindra*. This hinders the perception of complete substance.

vii. **Prachala**: It is also one sort of slumber. When someone gets sleep in standing or seated form, it is known as *prachala*. This sleep hinders perception of complete substance.

viii. **Prachala prachala**: It is also one sort of sleep only. When someone gets sleep while walking also, then it is known as *prachala prachala*. This sleep hinders perception of complete substance.

ix. **Thinidhi**: This is also one sort of sleep in which the strength of the person is similar to half- *chakri* strength in which the work desired during the day is being done at night. The person stays awake, finishes his day desired work and again goes to sleep, but in the morning he doesn't know that he has completed the work in the night is known as *Thinidhi*.

3. **Mohaniya Karma** (*Deluding Karma*):

It has 2 folds:

1. *Darshan mohaniya karma.*
2. *Charitramohaniya karma.*

i. **Darshan mohaniya Karma** is equal to drinking wine by which the soul gets confused and deluded about right and wrong belief. This is the first type of *Mohaniya Karma* known as *Darshan Mohaniya Karma*.

It has 3 folds:

a) ***Mithyatvamohaniya Karma:*** Due to outcome or effect of this *Karma*, there is no predilection for right tenets or right elements (*tatvas*) told by *paramatarka tirthanker parmatma*. This is the monarch of entire stack of *ashubha* (*evil*) *Karma*, the intense foe of the soul.

b) ***Mishramohaniya Karma:*** *Mishra* means mix. Due to outcome or effect of this *Karma*, there is neither predilection nor dislike for right tenets as told by *tirthanker parmatma*.

c) ***Samayak mohaniya Karma:*** Due to outcome or effect of this *Karma*, there is predilection for right tenets and right elements (*tatvas*). It is being acquainted as " *Samayak Darshan*"

ii. ***Charitramohaniya Karma:*** Means right conduct obstructing *Karma*. The person knows what is right and wrong. There is no delusion in belief but due to this *Karma* he is not able to execute what is right and beneficial for oneself.

The charitramohaniya Karma has 25 folds:

i. 16 *kashay*

ii. 9 *no-kashay*

Kashay means passion which has four folds.

i. Anger *krodh*

ii. Ego *Maan*

iii. Deceit *maya*

iv. Avarice *lobh*

These four fold *kashay's* are of different intensities which have four folds.

1. *Anantanubandhi kashay*
2. *Apratyakhyani kashay*
3. *Pratyakhyani Kashay*
4. *Sanjwalan Kashay*

1. **Anantanubandhi kashay:** *'Anant'* means infinite and *'bandhi'* means bonds. This *Karma* bonds the soul for infinite period of time in this *sansar*. This *Anantanubandhi* 4 kashay is the paramount cause for eternal *sansar* of soul.

2. **Apratyakhyani kashay:** *Pratyakhyan* means vows, pledges. 'A' denotes 'no'. Thus *apratayakhyani kashay* does not allow to accept a sole vow.

3. **Pratyakhyani kashay:** It allows accepting vow of *shravak dharma* but desists performing *sadhu dharma* ascetic vow is known as *pratyakhyani kashay*.

4. **Sanjwalan kashay:** This *kashay* does not impede taking *sadhu (ascetic) dharma* pledge but it slightly smears the pledge due to transgression.

We have perceived the different intensities of passion, so now we see the nature or trait of these four passions according to its intensities:

Four sorts of *krodh* (anger):

1. **Sanjwalan anger:** First the intensity of anger in *sanjwalan* category is akin to a line in water. As you draw a line in water and in the next second it gets rubbed. Similarly, the anger of *sanjwalan* gets cooled in a fraction of time.

2. **Pratyakhyani anger:** It is akin to a line in sand means the line drawn in sand gets rubbed out with a blow of wind; similarly the anger of *pratyakhyani* gets off with less effort.

3. **Apratyakhyani anger:** It is akin to a split in an earth means when there is a split in an earth it gets joined after rainfall. Similarly, the anger of *apratyakhyani* too gets serene cool after some more efforts.

4. **Anantanubhandhi anger:** It is akin to a split in mountain means the split in mountain doesn't get joined by any attempt.

Similarly, the anger of *anantanubandhi* too doesn't get serene by any efforts.

Four sorts of *Krodh* mentioned above are respectively more intense and sabotage the virtues of soul i.e. forgiveness.

Four sorts of *Maan* (conceit):

1. *Sanjwalan Maan*: It is akin to stick of cane. Means the stick of cane when bended can be straightened with no efforts. Similarly the *Maan* of *sanjwalan* can be washed off from the mind very soon.

2. *Pratyakhyani Maan*: It is akin to wood. As the wood can be bended slowly, similarly, the *Maan* of *pratyakhyani* can be renounced with some effort.

3. *Apratyakhyani Maan*: It is akin to bones. Means bones need more acute efforts to bend; similarly the *Maan* needs lot of efforts to relinquish.

4. *Anantanubandhi Maan*: It is akin to stone pillar. Means we can't bend the pillar of stone with any efforts. Similarly, the *Maan* of *anantanubandhi* can't be renounced by any efforts; it lasts long forever.

Four sorts of *Maan* conceit mentioned above are respectively more intense and sabotage the virtues of soul i.e. courtesy, relent, politeness, down to earth, etc.

Four sorts of *maya* (deceit)

1. ***Sanjwalan maya*:** It is akin to wooden chaff means the scrape of wooden can be curved and it gets straight with no efforts, similarly, the *sanjwalan* deceit gets abandoned very easily.
2. ***Pratyakhyani maya*:** It is akin to flow of urine of cow. As the *dhara* (flow) of urine of cow is crooked when strong wind blows but the crookedness disappears and flow becomes straight when the wind stops blowing. Similarly, the *maya* of *pratayakhyani* gets renounced by some efforts.
3. ***Apratyakhyani maya*:** It is akin to horns of goat. It is difficult to straighten the horns of goat. Similarly, the *maya* of *apratyakhyani* requires a sturdy effort to relinquish.
4. ***Anantanubandhi maya*:** It is akin to sturdy roots of bamboo. The roots of bamboo can't be made straight by sturdy efforts also. Similarly, the *maya* of *anantanubandhi* can't be demolished with any efforts.

The four sorts of *Maya* mentioned above are respectively more intense and sabotage the virtues of soul i.e. candour, straight forwardness, frankness etc.

Four sorts of *lobh* (avarice):

1. ***Sanjwalan lobh*:** It is akin to colour of turmeric. As the colour of turmeric gets faded when presented to the sun, the *sanjwalan lobh* too gets faded with no efforts.

2. ***Pratyakhyani lobh:*** Avarice it is akin to collyrium. As the spot of collyrium on cloth gets removed with few efforts, the *lobh* of *pratyakhayani* gets faded with few efforts.

3. ***Apratyakhyani lobh:*** It is akin to the grease of bullock cart. As the spot of grease requires more efforts to remove, the *lobh* of *pratyakhyani* requires more efforts to remove.

4. ***Anantanubandhi lobh:*** It is akin to crimson colour. As the cloth gets torn but the colour doesn't get faded at all, the *anantanubandi lobh* too doesn't get faded by any efforts.

Four sorts of *Lobh* mentioned above are respectively more intense and sabotage the virtues of soul i.e. generousness, magnanimous, open handed, etc.

Hence, these were the 16 *kashays* of *Charitramohaniya Karma*.

No Kashay:

9 no-*kashay* confer one's own effect when they are related to *kashay*. These no-*kashay* stimulates the *kashay*, increases *kashay* and inspires *kashay*;

Which are:

i. ***Hasya:*** Due to effect of this *Karma*, we feel like laughing *hasya* with reason or without any reason also.

ii. ***Rati:*** Due to effect of this *Karma*, we get attracted towards external and internal objects.

iii. ***Arati:*** Due to effect of this *Karma*, we feel repulsion towards external and internal objects.

iv. ***Bhaya:*** Due to effect of this *Karma*, we get afraid *bhaya* with reason or without any reason also.

v. **Shoka:** Due to effect of this *Karma*, we get grief *shoka* with reason or without reason also.

vi. **Jugupsha:** Due to impact of this *Karma*, we have strong dislike *jugupsha* towards filthy objects.

vii. **Striveda:** Due to impact of this *Karma*, the female (*stri*) kindles to have sexual relation with male.

viii. **Purushveda:** Due to impact of this *Karma*, the male (*purush*) spurs to have sexual relation with female.

ix. **Napunsak veda:** Due to impact of this *Karma*, the impotents covet to have sexual relation with both male and female.

4. **Antray Karma** (*obstructive Karma*): means by which the powers of liberality, etc, get restrained and do not bear fruit is obstructive *Karma*, resembling a store keeper.

Antray Karma has five folds:

- **Danaantray Karma:** *Alms obstructive Karma*
- **Labhaantray Karma:** *Gain obstructive Karma*
- **Bhogaantray Karma:** *Enjoyment obstructive Karma*
- **Upbhogaantray Karma:** Re-enjoyment obstructive *Karma*
- **Viryaantray Karma:** Strength power obstructive *Karma*

   i. **Danaantray Karma:** Dana means 'alms', 'to impart.' The person may possess competent substances to give alms, to impart, there may be competent and pious souls present to receive and further more he has acquainted that to impart competent substances to pious souls (*supatra*) is for utmost fruits. Yet, he does not have zeal to alms; to impart this is the outcome of *danaantray Karma*.

ii. **Labhaantray Karma:** 'To obtain', 'to procure' is known as *labha*. The person who is competent and pleased to confer; the competent person is prepared to receive, to gain; yet he cannot gain is outcome of *labhaanatray Karma*.

Labha means 'to gain', *Antray* means 'to obstruct', barrier, means obstruction in gaining, obtaining any substances.

iii. **Bhogaantray Karma:** 'To consume', 'to devour'. Special dishes are prepared, the person is not having penance *tapa* then also he or she cannot consume or devour due to some reasons like health, time etc is all due to *bhogaantriya Karma*.

Bhoga means to consume, to devour; *antray* means obstruction in consuming perishable substance.

iv. **Upbhogaantray Karma:** 'To consume a substance anew'. The substances which can be consumed frequently are present, are gained and you do not have any vow or penance then also you cannot consume the substance one or more times is outcome of *upbhogaantrya Karma* i.e. garbs, utensils, female, jewelry, etc

Upbhoga means to consume again and again.

Antray means to obstruct, obstruction in consuming non perishable substance again and again.

v. **Viryaantray Karma** *(strength)*: The person possess healthy physique, youthfulness then also who lacks in strength, does not activate one's own youth and are also not zealous to activate one's own youth is the outcome of *viryaantray Karma*.

5. **Vedaniya** *(feeling)* **Karma** *has two folds:*

i. *Shata vedaniya Karma:* It imparts peace and good health.

ii. *Ashata vedaniya Karma:* It imparts pain and suffering.

Resembling tasting the edge of a sword blade smeared with honey. As first, it confers joy and in a fraction of time confers pain too.

6. **Aayushya** (*age Karma*) *has four folds:*

    i. Human beings

    ii. Animal beings

    iii. Celestial inhabitants

    iv. Hell inhabitants

Aayushya holds the creatures in their respective birth according to their life span. It is like a prison.

7. **Gotra Karma** (*Family determining Karma*) *has two folds:*

    i. High family determining *Karma* (*uchh* gorra)-birth in higher levels of life

    ii. Low family determining *Karma* (*nich gotra*)-*birth* in low and stooping levels of life.

Family determining *Karma* causing high or low family is like a potter making milk vessels and wine-vessels.

   i. **High family determining Karma:** This *Karma* imparts supreme gender, family, strength, beauty, penance, knowledge, opulence etc.

   ii. **Low family determining Karma:** The outcome of this *Karma* is that even though the person possesses good knowledge and a pious soul, he is rewarded with hatred.

8. **Nam Karma** (*body making Karma*) which has 93 folds and confers difference in the condition of body like a painter. It imparts different sorts of bodies to creatures.

Total *Nam Karma*	**93 folds**
14 pinda prakruti	*65 folds*
28 pratyek prakruti	*28 folds*

14 *pinda* combined *prakruti*:

1.	Gati Karma	:	4 folds
2.	Jati Karma	:	5 folds
3.	Sharir Karma	:	5 folds
4.	Aangopanga Karma	:	5 folds
5.	Bandhan Karma	:	5 folds
6.	Shanghatan Karma	:	5 folds
7.	Sansthan	:	6 folds
8.	Shanghayan	:	6 folds
9.	Varna	:	5 folds
10.	Gandh	:	2 folds
11.	Ras	:	5 folds
12.	Sparsh	:	8 folds
13.	Aanupurvi	:	4 folds
14.	Vihayo gati	:	2 folds
	Total *pinda prakruti*	:	65 folds

28 *pratyek prakruti*	**28 folds**
Independent *prakruti*	8 folds
Trasadasak	*10 folds*
Sthawardasak	*10 folds*

28 *pratyek prakruti* of which 8 are independent:

i. Paraghata Nam Karma

ii. Uchhwasa Nam Karma

iii. Aatap Nam Karma

    iv. Udhyot Nam Karma

    v. Agurulaghu Nam Karma

    vi. Tirthanker Nam Karma

    vii. Nirman Nam Karma

    viii. Upghat Nam Karma

10 *Trusadasaka Nam Karma:*

    i. Trasa

    ii. Badar

    iii. Paryapti

    iv. Pratyek

    v. Sthir

    vi. Shubha

    vii. Suswara

    viii. Soubhagya

    ix. Aadeya

    x. Yash

10 *Sthawardasak Nam Karma:*

    i. Sthawar

    ii. Sukshma micro

    iii. Aparyapti

    iv. Sadharan comman

    v. Asthira unstable

vi. *Ashubha*

vii. *Durbhagya*

viii. *Duswara*

ix. *Anadey*

x. *Apayash*

Let's elucidate 14 *pinda prakruti* which has 65 folds:

1. **Gati Nam Karma: (4 folds)**

Following 4 phases are achieved due to *Gati Nam Karma:*

　　i. Human being *Gati Nam Karma Aayushya Gati*

　　ii. Celestial being *Gati Nam Karma Dev Gati*

　　iii. Hell being *Gati Nam Karma Narak Gati*

　　iv. Animals being *Gati Nam Karma Tiryanch Gati*

2. **Jati Nam Karma: 5 fold:** *Jati* means gender

　　i. One senses gender *ekindriya* e.g. stones, water, air, fire and all types of flora.

　　ii. Two senses gender *beindriya* e.g. earthworm, conch, worms etc.

　　iii. Three senses gender *teindriya* e.g. ant, louse, bug etc.

　　iv. Four senses gender *chauindriya* e.g. fly, butterfly, mosquito etc.

　　v. Five senses gender *panchindriya* e.g. human beings, animals, hell inhabitants and celestial inhabitants

This *Jati* gender is gained according to *Jati* gender *Nam Karma*

3. **Sharir Nam Karma: (5 folds)**

    i. *Audarik Sharir* (body)

    ii. *Vaikriya Sharir* (body)

    iii. *Aaharak Sharir* (body)

    iv. *Tejas Sharir* (body)

    v. Karman Sharir (body)

    i. **Audarik Sharir:** Due to effect of this *Karma*, the soul gathers *Audariksharir* apt matters and constructs *audariksharir* e.g. Human body and animal body are known as *Audarik sharer*.

    ii. **Vaikriya Sharir:** Due to effect of this *Karma*, the soul gathers *vaikriya sharir* apt matters and constructs *vaikriya sharir* e.g. hell and celestial inhabitants.

    The matters of these both bodies are *vaikriya* matters.

    iii. **Aaharak Sharir:** Due to effect of this *Karma*, the soul gathers *aaharak sharir* apt matters and constructs *aaharak sharir*.

    iv. **Tejas Sharir:** Due to effect of this *Karma*, the *tejas sharir* apt matters are being gathered by soul and converts into *tejas sharir*. This *sharir* digests the food; it is being possessed by every *sansari* soul. This *sharir* keeps warmness in *audarik sharir*

    Due to this *sharir* all soul's body temperature is in control. This *sharir* controls the temperature of all living beings hence when the living being dies, the body of living being gets cool.

    v. **Karman Sharir:** Due to effect of this *Karma*, the *Karman sharir* apt matters are being gathered by soul and converts into *Karman sharir*. This *sharir* is being possessed by every *sansari* soul and it is carried forward in other incarnations too.

4. **Aangopanga Nam Karma: (5 fold)**

   i. *Audarik Angopanga*

   ii. *Vaikeriya Angopanga*

   iii. *Aharak Angopanga*

   i. **Ang:** Body 'organs' i.e. head, chest, stomach, back, 2 legs and 2 hands.

   ii. **Upanga:** Organ's 'organs' *upanga* i.e. Head's organs, eyes, nose, ear etc.

   iii. **Aangopanga:** The minor organs of major organs. Like sub organs of eyes are eyelids, eyelashes etc, these are *Aangopanga*.

5. **Bandhan Nam Karma:(5 Folds)**

The matters of different *sharir* which have been already taken and new one which are taken in present are being joint together due to this *Bandhan Nam Karma* known as *Bandhan Nam Karma*.

This has 5 folds:

   i. *Audarik bandhan Nam Karma*

   ii. *Vaikriya bandhan Nam Karma*

   iii. *Aharak bandhan Nam Karma*

   iv. *Tejas bandhan Nam Karma*

   v. *Karman bandhan Nam Karma*

   i. **Audarik bandhan Nam Karma:** The *audarik* matters which have been taken before and new one which is being taken in present in every sole-second are joint together due to this *Karma*, known as *audarik bandhan Nam Karma*. The definition of 2nd, 3rd, 4th and 5th *bandhan Karma* is respectively same as *audarik bandhan*.

6. **Shanghatan Nam Karma: (5 folds)**
    i. *Audarik shanghatan Nam Karma*
    ii. *Vaikriya shanghatan Nam Karma*
    iii. *Aaharak shanghatan Nam Karma*
    iv. *Tejas shanghtan Nam Karma*
    v. *Karman shanghatan Nam Karma*

    i. **Audarik Shanghatan Nam Karma**: To construct *audariksharir*, how much stock of *audarik* matters *pudgala* will be needed is being decided by this *Karma* and also *pudgala* are being compressed to form *audarik sharir*. The definition of the other four *bandhan Karma* is respectively same as *shanghtan Nam Karma*.

7. **Sansthan Nam Karma: (6 folds)**

The shape or figure of body:

   i. *Samchatursra sansthan*
   ii. *Nyagrodh sansthan*
   iii. *Sadi sansthan*
   iv. *Kubja sansthan*
   v. *Vaman sansthan*
   vi. *Hundak sansthan*

   1. **Samchaturasra**: In this seating position *sansthan*, the distance between right knee and left shoulder, distance between left knee and right shoulder, distances between both knee and head is similar, perfectly symmetrical physique that is known as *Samchaturasra sansthan* (*shape of body*).

2. **Nyagrodh:** In this *sansthan,* the organs above navel are completely in proportion but organs which are below navel or torso does not correspond is known as *nyagrodh sansthan.*

3. **Sadi:** In this *sansthan,* the organs below navel are completely in proportion but organs above navel are not in proportion is known as sadi *sansthan.*

4. **Kubja:** In this, head, neck, hand and legs are completely in proportion and chest, stomach etc. are not in proportion is known as *Kubja* i.e. Hunchback.

5. **Vaman:** In this, chest, stomach etc. are in proportion but head, neck, hand and legs etc. are not in proportion. This is known as dwarfish *vamansansthan,*reverse of *kubja.*

6. **Hundalc:** In this, overall organs of body are not in proportion, deformed nor have good features is known as *hundak sansthan.*

8. **Sanghayan Nam Karma: (6 folds)** the strength and structures of bones.

   i. *Vajrarishabhnarach sanghayan*

   ii. *Rishabhnarach sanghayan*

   iii. *Narach sanghayan*

   iv. *Ardhnarachsanghayan*

   v. *Kilika*

   vi. *Chhevattu*

   i. **Vajrarishabhnarach sanghayan:**

   '*Vajra*' means needle of bone.

   '*Rishabh*' means collar or binding to cover the bone.

'*Narach*' means double mortise as the child of monkey is attached to her mother.

In this *sanghayan,* the strength and structure of the bone are healthy and powerful. In this, the bones are joined to each other as the child of monkey is joined to her mother and on that the binding of bones is there and in middle of that the needle of bones has been pierced. This sort of bone strength is known as *vajrarishabhnarach sanghayan*. The strength of bones in this *sanghayan* is more than iron strength.

ii. ***Rishabhnarach sanghayan:*** *In this sanghayan*, there is *narach* i. e. double mortise on both sides. On that there is a binding of the bone which is known as *rishabhnarach sanghayan.*

iii. ***Narach sanghayan:*** The two bones are joined as *narach*; there is neither binding nor needle in the *narach sanghayan.*

iv. ***Ardhnarach sanghayan:*** '*Ardh*' means half. '*Narach* means joint of bones mortise is only on one side; and on the other side only needle is being pierced. This *sanghayan* is known as *ardh narach sanghayan.*

v. ***Kilika:*** '*Kilika*' means needle. The bones are only being joined with *kilika needle* in *kilika sanghayan.*

vi. ***Chhevattu:*** In this *sangyahan,* the ends of bones are only touching each other. '*Chhevattu*' means *chheda* which means 'end' where end of the bones are just touching each other.

9. ***Varna Nam Karma:*** **(5 Fold)** 'Varna' colour of body.

   i. Green colour. Due to this *Karma,* you gain green complexion e.g. emerald.

   ii. Red colour. Due to this *Karma,* you gain red complexion e.g. cinnabar.

   iii. Yellow colour. Due to this *Karma,* you gain yellow complexion e.g. turmeric.

iv. White colour. Due to this *Karma*, you gain white complexion e.g. pearls.

   v. Black colour. Due to this *Karma*, you gain black complexion e.g. black pepper stone.

10. **Gandh Nam Karma: (2 fold)** *Gandh* means the smell or odour of the body.

    i. ***Sugandh Nam Karma***: e.g. good odour of body. E.g. camphor

    ii. ***Durgandh Nam Karma***: bad odour of body. E.g. garlic

11. **Ras Nam Karma: (5 fold)** *Ras* means the taste of body.

    i. ***Tikt chilly ras*:** Due to this *Karma*, the body gets chilly *ras* e.g. chilly.

    ii. ***Madhur sweet ras*:** Due to this *Karma*, the body gets sweet *ras* e.g. sugarcane.

    iii. ***Katu bitter ras*:** Due to this *Karma*, the body gets bitter *ras* e.g. *neem* tree.

    iv. ***Kashayras*:** Due to this *Karma*, the body gets *kashayras* e.g. hog plum.

    v. ***Aamla sour Ras*:** Due to this *Karma*, the body gets sour *ras* e.g. tamarind.

12. **Sparsh Nam Karma: (8 folds)** *Sparsh* means touch of body.

    i. ***Mrudu smooth* touch:** Due to this *Karma*, body gets smooth touch e.g. flower.

    ii. ***Karkash rough* touch:** Due to this *Karma*, body gets rough touch e.g. stone.

    iii. ***Guru heavy* touch:** Due to this *Karma*, body gets heavy touch e.g. iron.

iv. **Laghu** *light* **touch:** Due to this *Karma*, body gets light touch e.g. cotton.

v. **Snigdh** *sticky* **touch:** Due to this *Karma*, body gets sticky touch e.g. butter, honey.

vi. **Ruksh** *non-sticky* **touch:** Due to this *Karma*, body gets non sticky touch e.g. ashes.

vii. **Ushna** *hot* **touch:** Due to this *Karma*, body gets hot touch e.g. fire.

viii. **Sheet** *cold* **touch:** Due to this *Karma*, body gets cold touch e.g. ice.

13. *Aanupurvi Nam Karma*: (4 folds)

    i Human *Aanupurvi*

    ii. Celestial *Aanupurvi*

    iii. Hell *Aanupurvi*

    iv. Animal *Aunupurvi*

14. *Vihayo Gati*: (2 folds) means 'gait' i.e. style of walking.

    i. Good gait

    ii. Bad gait

The 14 *pinda parkrutis* clarification is over.

8 *pratyek Nam Karma*: *'Pratyek'* means independent fold.

1. *Paraghata Nam Karma*: Due to effect of this *Karma*, the soul by his personality agitates others and he himself doesn't get agitated by other's personalities.

2. *Uchwasa Nam Karma*: Due to effect of this *Karma*, the soul gets power to breathe smoothly.

3. **Aatap Nam Karma:** Due to effect of this *Karma*, the cool body of the soul confers warm light e.g. *badar pruthavikaya* body i.e. sun.

4. **Udhoyat Nam Karma:** Due to effect of this *Karma*, the cool body of soul confers cool light. E.g. *badar pruthavikaya* i.e. moon, stars, planets.

5. **Agurulaghu Nam Karma:** Due to effect (*uday*) of this *Karma*, the body of soul is proportionate.

6. **Tirthanker Nam Karma:** Due to effect of this *Karma*, the soul becomes *Tirthanker* in last incarnation.

7. **Nirman Nam Karma:** Due to effect of this *Karma*, the soul gains body with proper organs and in appropriate place.

8. **Upghath Nam Karma:** Due to effect of this *Karma*, the soul bears pain due to one's own body organs e.g. tumour, etc.

The 8 *pratyek prakrut* classification is over.

10 **Trasadasak Nam Karma:** '*Trasa*' means *movable*, '*dasak*' means *ten*. e.g. Two, three, four and five senses species have *trasa Nam Karma*.

   i. **Trasa:** means *movable* which can move as per own wish i.e. movable souls.

   ii. **Badar:** means *gross*, which can be seen by naked eyes.

   iii. **Paryapti:** Due to effect of this *Karma*, the soul can complete own *paryapti*.

   iv. **Pratyek:** Each and every soul possesses his own personal body.

   v. **Sthir:** The organs of the body are stable e.g. teeth, bones etc.

vi. **Shubha**: Due to effect of this *Karma*, the upper organs of body are fit and appropriate.

vii. **Suswara**: Due to effect of this *Karma*, the soul gains melodious sound which enchants others.

viii. **Soubhagya**: Due to effect of this *Karma*, if the soul doesn't do philanthropy on others then also he is loved by everyone.

ix. **Aadeya**: Due to effect of this *Karma* even if the language of a person is harsh, then also he is loved by everyone.

x. **Yash**: Due to effect of this *Karma* the soul gains fame and is renowned in the universe.

10 Sthawardasak Nam Karma: 'Sthawar' means the living beings which cannot move as per their own wish i.e. immovable living beings and 'dasak' means ten e.g. one sense species.

i. **Sthawar**: Due to effect of this *Karma*, the living beings cannot move as per their own wish. They are immovable souls.

ii. **Sukshma**: Due to effect of this *Karma*, the body obtained by the soul is not visible by naked eyes.

iii. **Aparyapti**: Due to the effect of this *Karma*, the *paryapti* of the soul is not complete.

iv. **Sadharan common**: Due to effect of this *Karma*, infinite souls get a common body.

v. **Asthira**: Due to effect of this *Karma*, the organs of physique are unstable.

vi. **Ashubha**: Due to effect of this *Karma*, the lower organs below navel are deformed.

vii. **Durbhagya**: Due to effect of this *Karma*, if the soul does philanthropy towards others then also that soul is not loved by others.

viii. ***Duswara*:** Due to effect of this *Karma*, the soul gets bad sound.

ix. ***Anadeya*:** Due to effect of this *karma*, even if the soul speaks the truth, no one likes or appreciates it. He is not liked or loved by people.

x. ***Apayash*:** Due to effect of this *Karma*, the soul gains obscurity and no credit in world.

The characteristics of entire 8 *Karmas* and sub factors of 8 *Karmas* have been decoded. Hence, we comprehend that the *Karmas* are smudge on the soul and are 'heya' (*to be renounced*) and now we dwell on the causes how each *Karma* gets bonded with soul. Thus, we can have precautions to hinder its influx towards the soul.

1. **Causes of *gyan avarniya Karma bandh* and *darshan avarniya Karma bandh*:**

By doing contempt towards *gyan* (*knowledge*), *gyanis* (*erudite knowledgeable personalities*); devices of *gyan*, e. g. books, pen, pencil, paper in any form, etc.; and devices of *darshan*, e.g. *sadhu, sadhvi,* icon of God, ethics etc.

Following are different sorts of *aashatnas* of *gyan* and *darshan*, which result into the *Gyan avarniya* and *Darshan avarniya Karma bandh:*

1. To have feelings of enmity towards *gyan, gyanis, darshan* and devices of *gyan* and *darshan*.

2. To have contempt towards *gyan, gyanis, darshan* and devices of *gyan* and *darshan*.

3. To laugh or slander or be envious of *gyanis*.

4. Not having faith on *Gyani's* and doubting their words.

5. To have indolence for learning *gyan*.

6. To burn any sorts of paper, take any sorts of papers in washroom, eat on paper, clean the hands and filth with papers, sit on paper, wear the garbs having words on it, etc.

7. Intentionally not to impart *gyan* devices to other aspirant personalities.

8. If we have *gyan* of any subject but due to indolence we do not impart to other intrigued personalities.

9. We have knowledge of any sort of complicated subject but we do not impart to other intrigued persons with the intent that they will overcome us in knowledge and it may result into loosing of our importance.

10. To forget religious *gyan* due to lack of revision.

11. To obstruct in gaining food, garbs, place, devices of *gyan* etc. to intrigued personality.

12. The intent of ignorance

13. Having *kashay* is also a cause for *gyan avarniya* and *darshan avarniya Karma bandh*.

2. **Causes of *Mohaniya Karma bandh*:**

   a) **Causes of *darshan mohaniya Karma bandh*:**

   1. To impart preach of wrong path.
   2. To sabotage the right path.
   3. To take off the *deva dravya* i.e. money related to God reverence.
   4. To slander *tirthanker parmatma*.
   5. To slander *sadhu* and *sadhvi*.
   6. To slander the icon of God.
   7. To slander *sangha* (*sadhu, sadhvi, shravak and shravika*)

b) *Cause of charitramohaniya Karma bandh:*

The people who indulge in *Kashay* and *Naukashay* bind their souls with *Charitramohaniya karma*.

3. **Causes of** *Antray* (*obstructive*) *Karma bandh*:
   1. To hinder someone from doing worship of God and *Guru*.
   2. Personalities who are always alert to do violence, lies, stealing, non-celibate and possessions.

4. **Causes of** *shatavedaniya* **and** *ashatavedaniya Karma bandh*:

   Causes of *shatavedaniya Karma bandh*:
   1. Respect towards God and *guru:* '*Guru*' includes parents, tutors etc, who have obliged us.
   2. To forgive: If someone scorns on us, then also think that he is giving us chance for *nirjara* means which enhances our endurance power and curbs our state of mind; and due to that influx of *ashubha* evil *Karma* halt and the evil *Karma* which are in stock get detached from the soul. Hence, forgive them and ponder over the consequences of performing *kashay*.
   3. To have compassion (*daya*): To have compassion towards needy, destitute and unhappy souls is known as *dravya* compassion.

      Bhava daya means to have compassion towards ignorant and immoral souls; that they get free themselves from their evil deeds; and do endeavour to procure *dharma* knowledge.
   4. To take *Niyam*(pledge): To keep the reigns of the mind under full control by adhering to austerities and taking a lot of vows and pledges.
   5. To have *shubha yoga*: To halt *ashubha* deeds of *Maan* (*mind*), *vachan* (*speech*) and *kaya* (*physique*); and relate to *shubha* deeds which are devices to embark on *moksh*.

6. To have control over passions: To do endeavour for restraining all sorts of passions as they are paramount causes for enhancement of *sansar*, can be anger, conceit, deceit, greed, attachment, loath etc.

7. To confer *dana* (*alms*): To bestow alms can be *abhaydana* assurance of safety to living beings; *supatradana* alms to reverence personalities - sadhus, sadhvis, shravaks and shravikas; and *anucompadana* to give alms to destitute personalities.

8. Resolute mind in *dharma*: To be resolute while doing *dharma* and let adversities or tribulation occur while performing *dharma*.

Causes of *ashatavedaniya Karma bandh*:

The causes for bond of *ashatavedaniya Karma* are opposite of all causes of *shatavedaniya Karma* and in addition to impart unhappiness, to mourn, to lament, to slay, to agonies etc. towards any living beings.

To cut, to pierce the organs of animals, to use them as vehicles without compassion; to impart unbeneficial guidance, advice to others are also various causes for bond of *ashatavedaniya Karma*.

5. **Causes of *Aayushya Karma bandh*:**

There are four folds of *Aayushya Karma*:

1. ***Narak* (*Hell*) *Aayushya Karma*:**

   i. The person whose mind is tied with massive industrial, machinery activities and consistent thoughts are of economical devices.

   ii. The person whose mind is tied with how to accumulate possessions, how to escort them, how to increase them; and consistent pondering over them.

   iii. The person who does *raudra dhyan* (*evil mull*).

   iv. The person who has *mithyatva* (*strong wrong belief*) and has strong *anantanu bandh kasahays* (*intentions*).

2. **Causes of animal inhabitants *aayushya Karma* are:**

   i. The person who has deceit in heart

   ii. The person who differs in speech and heart

   iii. The person who has trickery in mind double dealing

   iv. The person who does fraud or cheating

3. **Causes of human inhabitants are:**

   i. By nature whose passion are cursory.

   ii. The person whose nature is generous to confer own money, garbs, land etc. to needy persons.

   iii. The person who possesses virtues like alms, compassion, philanthropy, etc.

   iv. *Samyagadrashti dev* and *narak* get birth as human beings.

4. **Causes of celestial inhabitants are:**

   i. *The samyagadrashti*, who perform penance, who does *akama nirajara*, *sadhu*, *sadhvi*, *shravak*, *shravika* who maintains *shubh dhyan* and *shubh leshya*.

6. **Causes of bond of *shubha Nam Karma*:**

   i. One who is candour and without deceit.

   ii. One who is without three *garava*.

   iii. *Garava* interpret for tempt, lure, sturdy attachment.

This has 3 fold:

- *Ras garava*
- *Ruddhi garava*
- *Shata garava*.

- *Ras garava:* who doesn't have lure, and sturdy attachment for sensual pleasure.

- *Ruddhi garava: ruddhi* means wealth opulence and it means who doesn't have lure, and sturdy attachment for wealth and opulences.

- *Shata garava:* who doesn't have lure and sturdy attachment for bliss devices.

Causes of *ashubha Nam Karma bandh:*

i. The deceit personalities, sweet in speech and bitter by heart.

ii. The person who has fervent feelings for enjoying five sensual objects and having consistent inclination for that.

iii. The person who possesses predilection-to gain money, to accumulate money, to increase money, and has consistent inclination for money.

8.1. Causes of *uchha gotra* (*high family determining*) **Karma bandh**:

i. The person who has predilection for *guna* virtues and have vision to perceive *guna* of other souls also.

ii. The person who confesses one's own minor faults also.

iii. The person who has abjured 8 folds of conceit *Maan*.

iv. The person who possesses sturdy feeling to gain true knowledge.

v. The person who has a great reverence towards God and *guru*.

2. Causes of bond of *nicha gotra Karma:*

i. The person who always beholds other's faults, weak points.

ii. The person who speaks about own virtues, and who hymns one's own virtues.

iii. The person who is indolent in procuring knowledge.

iv. Also without zeal to impart knowledge to others.

v. The person who does slander of God and *guru bhagwant* also.

vi. The person who have ego for all eight good things.

vii. The person who obstruct someone performing jina *pooja,* reverence of *guru* etc.

viii. The person who has passion for 18 *papsthanak*(devices for paap): 1. Violence 2. Lie 3. Stealing 4. Unchastity 5. Possessions 6. Anger 7. Conceit 8. Deceit 9. Avarice 10. Attachment 11. Loathing 12. Quarrel 13. Calumny 14. Roguery 15. Like, dislike 16. Slander 17. Lie with deceit 18. *Mithyatva shalya.*

Chapter 4

RAGA
THE INFECTED PHASE OF THE SOUL

RAGA MOHA MAMATA ATTACHMENT - VICE/VERSUS/*SAMATA* EQUANIMITY-VIRTUE

Raga, moha-mamta is one of the biggest vice of the soul and is the consequence of *mohaniya* karma. *Raga mohaniya* is the sub factor of *mohaniya* karma - the deluding *karma*. The true nature of this tactful *karma* is to delude the soul of its true and rightful tenets and its true qualities. It is the most disastrous *karma* because it perceptibly presents an inverted picture. The universal truth is presented wrongly. It is being presented and perceived wrong, for instance, the sensual pleasures and passions which are unbeneficial, harmful and confer agony to the soul in the long run.

They are presented delusively as if they are glamorous to the soul and the worst part is that the opposite of these vices i.e. the virtues which are really beneficial to the soul, the virtues confer autonomy and independence to the soul are presented as most unbeneficial and the giver of agonies! That is why *raga* is always called sugar coated. It acts sweetly but causes harm silently. The objects of joy of *mithyatwa mohaniya* are *vishay*, *vasana*, and pleasure from sensual objects, *kashays* or vices, and the lure of passions; all of which are the strongest enemies of the pure untarnished souls and all these are portrayed and presented as friends of the soul as the result of the perverse vision, the *'ultachasma'* or the inverted spectacles which has been adorned to us by *mohaniya* karma.

Raga mohaniya works in another way too. It hinders from exposing the supreme soul virtue- *vitaragata* or the non-attachment, which is the manifestation of the most upmost virtues of the soul without any sorts of passions. It is the complete detachment uprooting of *mohaniya karma* from the soul.

RAGA means attachment.	Where there is attachment, there is expectation
	Where there is expectation there is dependency
	Where there is dependency, there is agony
	As dependency co-exists with agony

Hence, the path to gain bliss and peace lies in abjuring and relinquishing the *raga* or the attachment for person and substance from our lives.

Raga mohaniya is the tumour root from which the seed of *sansar* or the mortal world of the soul sprouts and grows into a massive tree of 84 lakhs nuclei.

- The roots of a banyan tree start from a seed and slowly pervade and occupy a huge place and develop in a massive tree, in the same way, one seed of attachment paves way for umpteen roots and grows into a large massive tree, engulfing people in it by various sorts of attachments and relationship with other souls.

- The soul is born alone but the attachment and passion it develops for other souls and things are the causes for its future incarnations.

- The consideration and the delusion that this is my mother, father, sister, daughter etc and the *raga* feelings bestowed on them are reasons for infecting the soul with more and more attachment.

- Due to this vice of attachment, the person loses his power of discrimination between the right and the wrong as also the merits and the demerits. With the final results that the person indulges in any nefarious act for earning money for his family but does he realize that the people for whom he is doing the evil acts will not come with him, the evil effects of his deeds will haunt him in his next birth? *Raga* is thus declared as the mother of the entire *sansar*. The objects of *raga* may change but the negativity of the emotions will continue.

- We have heard people say love is blind. *Raga* is also a type of love and totally blind. What is the difference between a blind person and blind due to attachment? Well, a blind folded person cannot perceive who is in front of him or what is going in front of him but a person blinded by *raga* is unable to see anything because he chooses to be blind in his *raga* and he refuses to see anything beyond his attachment.

- The person, who is attracted by a woman, sees her as a thing of beauty, thinks her teeth are like flowers, her smile as heavenly, her face as a crescent of the new moon and her breast, which is just nothing but the compression of muscles, seems more alluring than a pitcher of gold. He seems to be lured and mesmerized and he doesn't realize that he is entering into a dangerous zone.

- The woman who is different in mind, speech and physique is also chaste for the person who is enticed due to his ardent emotions towards her.

- The personality, the figure of a woman is just a bundle of muscles, bones, blood, urine, excrement and phlegm overlapped by the cover of the skin. Hence, the affection towards her is mere fascination of attachment and attraction.

- It is this bond of attachment that makes the person foolishly consider all these unsecured relations as completely secure, all these transient relations as permanent and eternal. Discern this captivation of attachment; and you will find you are unable to come out of its fetters.

- See the stupor of attachment: a son filled with mud and filth comes and hugs his mother happily and the mother readily takes him in her arms, unhesitatingly and with willingness. The obstacle of mud, dirt and filth does not bother her and does not irritate her. This is the shrewdness of *raga*. It camouflages all other feelings and allows the attachment to reign supreme.

- Each and every soul is different from other souls as regards the *jad* part or the body part. Both, the soul and the body, are made up of different constituents. They cannot merge but the wily and cunning *raga* misleads the soul to accept the reverse; it bewitches the soul and makes it believe that this body is yours and everything related to the body is yours too. And the poor soul accepts this fact because he is subdued by *karma* but when it realizes the true facts, it becomes aware of the *'mayajaai'* of *raga*. Say a person sees a rod and mistakes it for a snake but when he realizes the true facts, the illusion is broken. In the same way, when the bewitchment of *raga* ends, real and true facts will surface out. When we realize that the soul is ours and much separate from the body, then slowly the attachment decreases and it gets nullified.

- *Raga* is the biggest foe for our soul as it deters our spiritual qualities and suppresses the original unattached nature. The *vitraagdasha* or phase of the soul shatters our virtues of true

- discrimination and curiosity which are very important to realize true visions, the real vision, and the ultimate goal of our human birth.

- Sometimes, in the course of our life, we may be filled with detachment and would want to partially or wholly renounce the world and move towards the path of salvation but if *raga kashay* is prominent, it would not allow us to do so. It will never allow us to retain the intensity of detachment and would try to take away the soul with various distractions and arguments-like, say, for instance, a father wants to take *'diksha* or complete renunciation', the *raga* will step in saying-"you have a responsibility towards your family" or "your wife is young. Who will look after her? The wicked world will eat her up" or "your sons are young. Who will look after them? They will go haywire" etc. They will hammer the poor soul so much that he will finally change his decision and will get caught again in the vicious circle of births and deaths. That is why *raga* is called sugar coated. It does its job but makes the person believe that it is for his or her own benefit. Now do you realize how cunning it is?

- It is amusing to see how the vice of attachment make you dance on its toes as it keeps the world revolving on its finger. Witness this scene: The son is suffering from cough and is unable to breath. The father puts his hand and pulls out the cough and if it still persists, he pulls it out with his own mouth. We would feel disgusting but the father is blind with his love. All he wants is to keep his child healthy and happy and he can go to any limits! This is the sad situation that *raga* puts us in. Not once but again and again we fall victim to the same blunder. In the next 20 years, if the situation reverses and the father suffers from the same disease, do you think his son will treat him well? In the same way as his father had done? All of us know the answer.

- We have now discerned all the characteristics of *raga*. Now, we are acquainted with its cunning nature, its alluring and misleading quality. It is then necessary for us to try and free ourselves from its clutches and move away from its allure. Practice the quality of *samta* or equanimity and yearn to move towards the true vision of our soul and try to uphold all our true virtues.

Samata or equanimity or non attachment

A real crystal is clear and transparent but when any coloured object is placed in front of it, it appears similar to the colour of the object.

When the object is removed, it then acquires its own pristine clear nature again. Exactly in the same way, when the soul is coloured with the colour of *raga* or attachment, it remains under its influence but once the object of *raga* or attachment is removed away from the vicinity of the soul, it regains its original equanimity quality. It proves that the equanimity or *samata* virtue of the soul endows calmness to mind and soul but it becomes overshadowed by the eclipse of *raga*, then *samata* becomes overshadowed.

Now, what is *samata*? What do we mean by it?

- It is the power to behave evenly in all circumstances and in all occasions with all people and with all living beings. Here's the description of *Samata*.
- It is the quality of bearing up all losses without a murmur and without losing hope.
- It is the ability to fight the bitterness of defeat and swallow it sweetly.
- It is the art of victory over anger under all contrasting situations.
- It is the ability to smile when tears are close to our eyes.

- It is the strength to resist all temptations towards evil and to forget revenge.

- It is to love the person who hates you or hurts you.

- It is to accept everything with a smiling face.

- It is to look on all living beings as equal and treat them the same.

- It is to behave with everyone in the same way as you would accept them to behave with you.

- The chances of attaining celestial joy are remote and so is the bliss of *Moksh* but the virtue of *samata* has the power to elate the mind and raise it to the level of these pleasures and that too in this birth itself. The abode of joy and happiness becomes lucid, acceptable and easily attainable.

- Is the idea of *Samata* clear? Well, it is the art of maintaining a status and a neutral reaction to every adverse action.

- It is the skill of contemplating welfare of one's own soul and that of all other souls.

- It is the feeling of equanimity of one's own soul compared with all other souls. No highs. No lows. Just as I love my soul, so do all other living beings.

- This feeling helps unfold the blind folded attachment. It cools off the heat of rage and consequently parcels off the excrement of rudeness and humiliation.

- The worldly *sansar* analogous to forest is burning in the fire of birth and death, of old age and unhappiness. *Samata* is a cooling ointment to ease the heat of sadness, from the pain and suffering, and from the attachment of relations. If any of our near and dear ones burns in this raging fire, we weep and repent the loss but *samata* helps us realize that all this is a part and parcel of life and all souls are immortal. What is burning in this raging fire are the mortal bodies.

- This paves way for the emancipation of the soul.
- Equanimity illuminates the path of *moksh*.
- Just as the collyrium stick, when applied to the eyes, it removes the faults from the eyes. Similarly, the divine stick of *Samata* when applied to our vision, removes vices and faults from the souls. The same faults which had so far camouflaged the real virtues and the real merits of our beautiful untarnished unstained soul.
- Even if the mind can temporarily be lured away from the pleasures of the mundane world, it can experience the ecstasy of equanimity and it can taste the nectar of *Samata* which is un-describable and not vocal to others but only the person experiencing it can realize it. Just as a virgin can never decipher the pleasure of copulation of other women with their spouses, in the same way, common people can never gauge the bliss of *samata* experienced by aspirant souls who are moving towards their goal of *moksh*.

The aspiration of being praised or received in the eyes of the beholders and of being famous, pierces the cores of the souls and causes infinite pain but the *samata* safeguards us from missing out our step, from slipping down the path of salvation. After all, the praise of the body is in actuality endangering to virtues of the soul. All our souls are detached from the body and all bodily feelings are harmful to the soul because they hamper the path towards salvation.

Just as the sun dispels darkness of night, *Samata bhav* aids in reducing the heap of *karma* accumulated by our soul and ensuring the illumination of the radiant soul within. All religious rituals should truly be done with the aim of imbibing the art of equanimity. If the religious rituals are performed with the intention of gaining praise and being magnified in the eyes of mortal men, then these acts stab and hurt our own soul. Such stabs do not encourage us towards *Nirjara* or partial detachment of these heaps of *karma*. Our final aim should be the complete emancipation of this *karma* from the souls.

Only if we perform all the religious rituals with this aim and with the aim of releasing the souls from the shackles of *karma,* only then they are truly performed rites, otherwise all our practices like *jap,* tap, and all penances, and all *aradhana* is just humbug because the true essence of religion is forgone. It is side geared and mere physical activities remain just as a full tank of muddy water, which can be cleaned by adding alum, exactly in the same way, the habit of *samata* or perfect balance of emotions can ensure pure joy, spiritual bliss, tranquility and ultimate peace and happiness. This is the magic wand of *samata*. It transforms you into a magical world of true and permanent tranquility, into the realm of true self-realization and the realization of the truth.

Chapter 5

ANGER-KRODH KASHAY
THE INFECTED PHASE OF THE SOUL

Anger is a passion which engenders due to *mohaniya karma*. It obstructs the virtue of forgiveness or *kshama* virtue of the soul.

Let's highlight the characteristics of this *Kashay*

- Anger is short time madness.
- Anger dwells only in the bosom of fools.
- If one is patient in one moment of anger, one will escape from a hundred days of sorrow.
- Whatever begins in anger ends in shame.
- The underlying cause of anger is an unfulfilled need.
- For every minute you are angry, you lose sixty seconds of your precious life.
- Anger arises from frustrated expectations.
- Anger begets a burning and scorching sensation to the soul.
- The aftermath of anger is birth in the inferno of hell and the resultant birth in animal incarnations. In short, human incarnation is lost and we lose the chance of begetting a human incarnation due to indulgence in anger.
- Anger disturbs our tranquility or peacefulness.

- Ego instigates anger.
- Anger is as deep as an ocean and as rapid as fire.
- Anger is always destructive, and forgiveness is always constructive and beneficial.
- Anger invites quarrels while forgiveness invites peacefulness.
- The antidote to anger is forgiveness. It is the only sure and safe remedy.
- Anger ends in spite, forgiveness leads to friendliness.
- Anger is alien to the soul, and forgiveness is a native of the soul.
- Anger kills and forgiveness saves.
- A small seed of anger can give birth to a huge tree of enmity.
- Many relationships, customers and friends are lost because of indulging in 'few minutes of an emotional bomb called anger'.
- Anger cannot be relinquished until one ousts the feelings of resentment. Only when one does this, anger disappears.
- Holding on to anger is like holding on to a burning coal with the intention of hurling it at someone but the holder gets burnt first.
- Spiritual seers therefore advice us to extinguish this fire of anger with the water of forgiveness. If we do not forgive, the anger and the hate continue down in the future births and can be the cause of unending births and deaths.
- The feeling of revenge evoked by anger is hard to cool down.
- Anger expressed causes hurt to others while suppressed anger can hurt us because it takes more energy to hold an emotion

than to release it. Continuous suppression leads to depression. Every time, when you are angry, acid is secreted in your body and the acid destroys the container that holds it. In the same way, every spell of anger affects and contaminates the soul. So, neither suppression nor expression is the solution. Transcending anger is the right solution.

- It is essential to understand the reason of anger. Anger is not a reaction to the world's behavior towards you; rather it is the frustration of not being able to get control of the situation.

- The remedy for conquering anger is being aware when anger crops up, ponder over the circumstances and ward it away. One minute of control can avoid the consequence of pain, sorrow and enmity. Slowly, the intensity of anger will decrease and anger will fade away and pave way for forgiveness and peace. Let awareness enter and let anger move out.

- If I allow the world to provoke me towards anger, it is worse than a dog being evoked to bark.

- Restraint can also help conquer anger. One can be careful to control it before its monstrous form emerges.

- Anger is like the acid that hurts, harms and affects the person who holds on to it rather than the one on whom it is targeted.

- The fire of anger destroys on its path all virtues like tranquility, harmony, piety, kindness, compassion, and pardon. The only way to get rid of this is to refrain from the terrible vice of anger.

Chapter 6

EGO-MAAN-KASHAY: THE INFECTED PHASE OF THE SOUL

Ego - The Perpetual Beggar

According to psychologists, ego is that part of a person's mind that tries to match the hidden desires of the unconscious mind with the desires of the real world. It is that part of the mind that mediates between the conscious and the unconscious, and is responsible for real testing and a sense of personal identity.

Ego is a passion *Maan-Kashay,* and a sub factor of *Mohaniya Karma;* thereby being rightly claimed as the monarch of entire universe.

It lives in an illusionary palace and tries all that is possible to maintain the facade of outward appearance.

Maan is that vice of the soul that hinders the virtues of humbleness, relentless, reverence and politeness.

It is easy to understand the concept of the whole universe but never the ego. We may be getting closer to the moon, but the self is more like a distant star for us.

- When ego enters, everything else goes, and vice versa.
- A heart filled with ego is always treading on the path of fire.

- The problem with ego is when ego is fed, one suffers a superiority complex. And when ego is starved, one experiences inferiority complex. Either way, it robs the composure of one's mind.
- There is not a moment of compatibility between ego and ease.
- Ego ruins reverence, courtesy, knowledge and benefits.
- Ego is simply an idea, an inflated image we carry of ourselves.
- The discriminating vision of a prudent person gets blinded due to their ego.
- The only positive thing about egoists is that they never talk about others. They are so engrossed and wrapped up in their own selves that for them, nobody else counts or matters.
- Ego pervades the creepers of demerits in one's life.
- Ego uproots the foundation of merit.
- Ego disturbs the composure of the mind!
- The price quoted by ego as motivator is the peace of our mind. "Why should we sell our hair to buy a comb?"
- Ego survives on the notion of self importance. It's a perpetual beggar asking for more and more; never satisfied with what it gets. It strives for more and more, basking in self esteem of rising above others and in other's eyes.

I am someone better…someone higher than the others. These are the perpetual thoughts plaguing our minds.

To be precise, it is the self esteem, or self image; the 'I' or the self of any person, his thinking, his believing, and his distinguishing itself from others. It is one's personal pride and self absorption and the feeling of gloating over others. It is the vice of conceitedness and self importance.

- When ego is done for gender, strength, beauty, penance, knowledge, caste or possessions in various incarnations, then in future births, all these are either denied or made available in lowly qualities. It is rightly said that pride comes before a fall. If you feel proud of any of your virtues, you are paving the way for its downfall in the future. But an egoistic person does not realize this till it is too late.

- Ego does not allow us to admit our mistakes. One considers it below their self esteem. 'I can never be wrong' is their prevalent attitude.

- Due to ego, we are constantly struggling to win over the situation...to be better than others.

- The flip side of ego is attention. Ego, for its existence, thrives on attention.

- Whatever ego does, it does it for being in the limelight. To get noticed, to be recognized, and to be appreciated are its main goals.

- It can be a good phase if we can transcend ego, try to win over ourselves, and make the best of our own potential.

Thus, all these are the characteristics and traits of ego. So, beware! Take double precaution, evade and get alert before the lightening of ego strikes on you. Stop the passion before it overtakes us, before it controls us!

In the process of feeding their ego, people hurt their near and dear ones. With the advent of ego, people behave in a way that makes them ashamed of their own actions in retrospect. This is because with ego; a human reacts like a completely insane and illiterate person in spite of all his education and wisdom. His actions no longer match either his social status or his qualifications. In the spur of a moment, all his reasoning powers evade him.

TO CONCLUDE-

There is enormous peace in letting your ego 'Go'.

The knack of rising above ego lies in the fact of comparing ourselves with people superior to us and those who have scaled greater heights than us.

Discipline and respect wins over 'EGO'.

Chapter 7

DECEIT - MAYA - KASHAY
THE INFECTED PHASE OF THE SOUL

What is deceit?

Deceit is purposeful falsehood.

It comes from the Latin word 'cheat'.

Deceit has a lot of meanings.

Deceit is the quality of being dishonest.

The art or practice of deceiving.

Concealment or distortion of truth for purpose of misleading. Perversion of truth for the purpose of misleading.

A tendency to cheat.

A trick to fool or mislead.

Hypocrisy in the pretence of possessing qualities of sincerity, goodness, devotion etc.

Giving a false impression to get away with something bad.

It is a quality of being fraudulent.

The quality of being crafty.

It is willful perversion of facts.

It is the double dealing of a person.

Another name for pretence.

It is the two faced personality of a person.

Can mean duplicity, trickery or hypocrisy.

Deceit is one of the vices or *doshas* of the soul which obstructs the quality or virtue of candour or truthfulness. Candour is in fact the doorway to *moksh*.

Deceit is very hazardous for our soul

- Deceit is the motherhood of *sansar*.
- Deceit is akin to a mythological monstrous planet causing eclipse in religious rites analogous to the moon.
- Deceit is the mainspring for disaster and calamities.
- Deceit is akin to fire for the creeper of *moksh*.
- Deceit is an obstacle for spiritual happiness.
- Deceit is the prime cause for bestowing female gender in the next birth.
- It can also be the cause for animal incarnations in next birth.
- Deceit is like a thunder bolt to the mountain of virtues.
- Deceit is a friend to direness and adversities.
- It is like adding more ghee to the lewdness of fire.
- Deceit is a burglar for the auspicious entry of knowledge.
- All penances and vows are rendered useless when they are camouflaged with deceit.

- If blindness is not treated, then the mirror is useless. Similarly, if deceit is not forsaken, then *dharma* and religious rituals are useless.

- Just as a single flaw makes all precious gems useless, in the same way the flaw of deceit renders all virtues meaningless.

- It may be possible to relinquish the taste of our buds to forsake the adornment of our body, but it is very arduous to oust the vice of deceit from our existence.

- Just as cold is a hindrance for lotus, fire for wood, night for day, folly for ethics, in exactly the same way hypocrisy is a hindrance for true *dharma*.

- Deceit encourages people to adorn the dress of an ascetic and deceive people and indulge in acts of trickery too. They burden their own soul and take along others in their doom.

- Deceit is a garb of pretence to win over the respect of others. It is a guise for the concealment of one's faults. Deceived people even adorn the clothes of saints to achieve their ends.

- These people can fool the world, but little do they realize that they are wounding their own soul by ousting the quality of honesty.

- Religion is a ship to cross the ocean of *sansar*. One must be very careful to see that there is no dent or hole if the ship is to successfully move forward. Religious rites are for the upliftment of the soul and it is necessary to be careful not to let vices like conceit to pierce it, otherwise the hot balloon of the upliftment of the soul will burst and come crashing down and all the efforts of lighting it would be lost in one sad moment.

- The instilling of deceit in religious initiation is like defiling one's own beauty of initiation and adorning it with filth.

- Deceit in this birth in religious activities particularly binds the soul in shackles of *karma* and will hinder him from begetting an apt incarnation to attain *moksh* in the next birth.

- Spiritual souls should ward off the traits of trickery and deceit. Only honest and candid souls are competent to relieve their souls from karmic bondage and reach the peak of salvation.

Chapter 8

AVARICE - LOBHA
THE INFECTED PHASE OF THE SOUL

All of us must have surely read the great *Ramayana*. As a story, it is an interesting one to listen. But as we grow up, the same story acquires different dimensions and perceptions. The story is about how a human being clings on to a certain thought, which he nourishes and feeds with more and more fuel, to turn into a vicious craving - a craving which soon acquired the form of a haunting demon. The demon first stirs the mind, disturbs it and finally controls it. It does not let the mind rest till the desire is fulfilled.

Take the case of *Ravana*. He was a great king. He had a kingdom brimming with wealth and prosperity. He was an ardent devotee of Lord *Munisuvrat Swami,* the *Tirthankar* of the *Jains* and performed rigorous penance and got the boon to rule all the three worlds. He possessed great knowledge of *jain* ethics, music and warfare. He had an enchanting and adorable wife named *Mandodari* and brave sons too. He had two dutiful brothers and one sister, *Surpanakha*. Everything was going on smoothly in his life till he heard about the fascinating *Sita Devi,* wife of *Rama*.

Surpanakha fed her brother's mind with descriptions of *Sita's* beauty, charm and her chiseled features. That did the trick. *Ravana* started fantasizing about her. Look at the irony. *Ravana* had not even had a glimpse of her but began yearning for her. He became restless with an overpowering desire to posses her. All the advices of his wife and brothers proved fruitless. He turned a deaf ear to their warnings and to the fact that she was someone's wife. When desire overtakes the mind, it stops discerning between the good and the bad, the right and the wrong.

Let's see the chain of events. A beautiful thing attracts one towards it. The mind appreciates it. The mind muses more and more over it. A craving to possess evolves. It becomes an obsession. The mind becomes a puppet in the hands of this obsession and finally loses its balance and sanity. The great demon of desire conquers the mind and all reasoning goes haywire.

To cut short a long story, and dwelling on matters of our concern, *Sita* was kidnapped and brought to *Ashoka Vatika* but being a pious lady, *Sita* refused his marriage proposal. *Ravana* became mad with rage and he began yearning for her even more. But *Sita* was a *'pavitra'* lady, who was only touched by her husband and no one else. As a result, *Ravana* decided to fight and kill *Rama*, so that *Sita* may have no other alternation but to marry him.

A battle ensued and *Ravana* lost so many of his family members, and his brother too joined the forces of Lord *Rama*. Despite being badly defeated, *Ravan* was not slain by Lord *Ram*, the embodiment of virtues, since he wanted *Ravana* to realize his folly but to no avail. *Ravana* finally lost the battle and his life too.

The story can teach us a lot. This is a good metaphor. In every human being there is *Rama* or the good thoughts and *Ravana* or the evil thoughts. It is up to us which to nourish and on which thoughts to dwell upon. It is in our hands to win over the evil thoughts without getting distracted by outer desires or objects of desire.

We must make our mind powerful to see through the *'Mayajaal'* or the hallucinations of desire. It is very important to dwell on our virtuousness and nourish it. It is equally necessary to recognize the friends and foes of our soul. It is really very important to see the realities and not be deluded by the hypnosis of avarice. Satisfaction is the greatest virtue of the soul. Remember one nourishes the soul and the other exploits. We must be diligent to recognize it. *Lobha* is the egg from which the endless births of *sansar* or the world will hatch. Our desires are controlled till they are in the shell of the satiety but once they hatch; they become bigger, stronger and uncontrollable. It is thus very imperative that we run away from the shackles of desires, from the prison of avarice and pave way for our own liberation. Liberation, as Oscar Wilde, the great writer puts it,

'The gates of hell are open night and day;

Smooth the descent and easy the way...

The gates of hell are three - Desire, anger, covetousness

The mind itself can make a heaven of hell and hell of heaven

The wicked go to hell, the righteous enter heaven.'

LOBHA-AVARICE- PRISONER OF DESIRE
INFECTION-DISEASE OF THE SOUL

Lobha is a never ending desire... The craving for more and more! It is the never ending craving for coveting more than what we have.

Right from childhood, we learn to yell and scream for what we want and this habit continues till the present day.

Today the reason for what we scream had changed.

But the yelling and yearning is perpetual.

Alas! Yearning and coveting is the root cause of all unhappiness.

Ponder over this.

When we were small, a tiny 60 rupees car was all we desired. We were satisfied on receiving it and playing with it. When it broke and fell, it caused us sadness but as we grew, our desire was upgraded to a 200 rupee remote controlled car. The same process continued till we got a battery operated car worth Rs. 20,000. The desire however never ceased with the price range escalating from 4 lakhs to 22 lakhs, to 36 lakhs and finally to a Ferrari, owned by very few people.

Did each possession give us joy? Did we ever contemplate on this? Every time something happened to the object of our pleasure, we became worried and unhappy with dissatisfaction creeping in. Objects keep changing but our greed keeps on increasing.

This is exactly the real face of *Lobha* or *Avarice*. One desire leads on to another, to another and the process moves on and on. There's no ending. Sadly our power of discernment didn't improve and we didn't learn from our mistakes. On the contrary, we became more and more involved with that object. One scratch on the car and our blood pressure is on the rise.

The yelling and craving has been prevalent at all times, the only change being that as we become older it becomes little sophisticated.

A wise man once threw down his toy himself, saying that "For 18 years, it has been giving me tension, the fear of breaking, the fear of being stolen, and the fear of it being mishandled. It is high time now to show who the master is."

The involvement and attachment of the temporal people to the sensuous pleasures, passions and positions are continuous.

Depending on the time, place, situation, the emotions, the cravings and yearning of objects and persons differ, but the feelings continue to rule. What is the quintessence behind all this?

The real fact is that each of these desires, these sensual pleasures and passions do not have the power to quench the greed and avarice of man. Ironically, they increase the longing, the thirst for more and more. If a person is thirsty and has only sea water around and were to drink that water, even a bucket full of sea water will not quench his thirst. But paradoxically, the same water will dry his throat and make him seek for more and more water resulting in vomiting, loose motions, uneasiness and the like. The secret behind this is that the pristine nature of sea water is unfit for satisfying the thirst.

Similarly the sensual, worldly pleasures can never quench our desires. The more we experience them, the more they disturb our peace of mind and stab the tranquility of the soul.

It is high time we realize the fact, that our soul is too precious for wasting on such temporary things.

It is high time we realize that it is not worth losing the tranquility of our soul for any of the worldly objects.

None of the worldly things give us peace. It is just a mirage of the mind. On the contrary, they evade our peace and bound the souls to innumerable births and deaths.

The more we stoop to lowly pleasures; we reserve our seats among the lowly creatures, the *'tiriyanch'*. The karmic matters gets accumulated on our souls, our birth into the low inhabitants becomes finalized. So intelligent and far sighted souls foresee the drastic consequences of giving vent to all such feelings and withdraw themselves at the right time from such snares of avarice and other vices because as we know prevention is better than cure. It is better to be cautious and safeguard one step rather than lament at leisure.

Chapter 9

JEALOUSY-ENVY
THE INFECTED PHASE OF THE SOUL

THE GREEN EYED MONSTER

This is one of the blemishes of the *soul-dosha-* which engenders the flawlessness of the soul.

Frankly, envy is a feeling of discontentment or resentment coming by someone else's possessions, feelings or luck.

Envy is a desire to have a quality, possession or any desirable thing belonging to someone else.

Jealousy or envy is a painful or resentful awareness of an advantage enjoyed by another joined with a desire to possess the same advantage. It is one of the negative emotions of living creatures which stirs and disturbs the composure of the soul.

There is just a slight difference between envy and jealousy; jealousy is the wish to keep what one has while envy is the wish to get what one does not have.

Let's articulate the manifold features of envy.

When someone has something that you don't possess or is able to build results that you are not able to build and unable to accept that fact, the resultant emotion is envy.

Envy is the pain that one arises by beholding the good fortune of others.

Envy uproots the roots of our existence and it gives rise to a feeling of irritation, aggravation, aggression and the soul is always restless. In actuality, it is sheer foolishness. It is comparing someone's outside with our inside and is highly dangerous for the soul because it gets inflamed in no time and that too for a worthless cause.

In the present scenario, the whole universe is full of unhappy people. Unhappy due to this negative attitude arising from this negative emotion of envy when even our food seems tasteless, our bread tasteless because we can't swallow the happiness bestowed on others as the negative emotions don't allow us to savour our good food. We constantly curse our luck and we are envious of the good luck of our opponents. What a sad situation! We can't eat the food laid on our plate and covet for the food in other's plate, which is not destined for us.

The most astounding fact is envy attacks us unarmed, suddenly, quickly and unannounced. We are caught unawares and we need strong will power to withstand its forces...

Envy operates subconsciously and is the cause for enormous stress.

Jealousy is worse than cancer because cancer destroys the cells of this body but consequences of envy proceed on to birth and after birth.

Envy, the green eyed monster, is the scariest of all creatures on this earth. It has devastated the virtuousness of hundreds of souls; it has ruined the healthy relationship between two people and caused havoc in the life of many souls.

Envy is even deadlier than greed because greed triggers a person to enrich himself but envy prompts him to deprive others.

Jealousy evokes emotions - the negative ones like rage, fury, embarrassment, sarcasm and the even more degrading feeling of inferiority complex.

It is a toxic emotion that corrodes it away from the inside and destroys our peace of mind.

The paradoxical aspect of envy is that we do not gain superiority over others because of our past *paap karma* and on the top of that we know that indignation and defiling in this birth deprives of these qualities in the next birth too. It results in the more and more decreasing of our *punya karma* and adding on to our *dosha karma* resulting in a pitiable state in the next birth.

The eradication and solution:

After having seen the devastating effects of envy, let us ponder on the solutions to eradicate this disease and renounce its negative propensity.

- The way to eradicate it is to find the root cause.
- What causes envy? It stems from a low self esteem.
- An idle mind is an abode of envy, negativity and its nourishment.
- The first and foremost solution is to starve it from negative thoughts and feed it with positive thoughts and the evil eyed monster will soon be choked when it will not get its feed.
- Surpassing negative emotions is not a permanent solution but a person must become aware of the thoughts thriving in his mind. He should introspect and ponder on its aftermath. He must realize that envy gains nothing. In fact, it takes away what you have; your own precious life. The invaluable human incarnation is lost and all for nothing. Think, realize and convince the mind of the worthlessness and slowly the intensity of these negative emotions will cease.

- The light of awareness is the only way to dispel the world of darkness created by envy.

- Envy thrives on comparison. Comparison is a boon and a bane. It can be used for our growth and at the same time, it can be the cause for our destruction.

- If we can use the powerful tool of envy for our growth for higher aspiration and for aspiring to become like the person we are envying, then it may be possible to surpass him. It can be a positive step. Rather than bringing him down, why don't we rise higher? The result can be wonderful and promising, right?

- The practice of praising another person is a great remedy to suppress envy. The habit of praising other's materialistic upliftment or emotional gain, love, affection, fame, goodwill, and status helps to shift our focus.

- Appreciating helps us to realize the good qualities and impede envy from flourishing. It helps to spurn envy from emerging in our mind and a healthy and competitive feeling emerges.

- The negative energy of envy can be utilized positively for the upliftment of our soul and transforming envy into growth is alchemy.

- Envy is a feeling which no one likes to admit and we always try to hide it from others but consequently, we end up hiding it from ourselves too as it proves to be treacherous for our own soul.

- The best remedy for envy is confession. Confess to your *guru* or mentor. It can be a great help to discuss it, ruminate on it, accept it, acquainted with it and finally neutralize it.

- While seething in envy, we tend to jeopardize the happiness of others and in the process we sabotage our own happiness too. When envy shows its evil face, we do not want anything for ourselves but are happy when the other person is deprived of what he has but with some analytical thing we can realize why we are forsaking our happiness at the cost of others. If he can be happy, why can't we too? Why to curse him? Why should someone else hinder our happiness? It is in our hands to make or mar our life.

- A talented person invites more envy from his peers than a wealthy person ever does; be generous and share your talents; you lose nothing as your gifts are imbibed in you.

- Envy is not an individual problem; it is a universal one. There is not a sole field, not even the spiritual one, who has not come in the clutches of envy. Envy is not mine or yours; we need the help of each other in tackling envy by helping others in overcoming envy, he is helping himself too.

- One of the ways to be free from the shackles of envy is to constantly express gratitude for our achievements, our good deeds and for all the good deeds done by others. A person who always expresses gratitude will be less attacked by negative emotions and his positivity will overtake the negativity as it is a great tool to manage the envy.

- Some frequently asked questions: what about envy caused by good luck?

  This is a tricky question. When our siblings, our relatives, good friends, who have never had the chance to be fortunate and suddenly when they rise in life and become rich and famous, then there is a perfect cause for envy to rise and to awaken envy. In such a case, the perfect remedy is to believe and accept that what he has achieved is the result of the *punya* accumulated in his last birth. The consequences of all the good acts that he has done in his past incarnations, he has sowed the seeds and he is now reaping fruits. Accept the fact that there is nothing superficial in this mundane world; everything works according to a fixed law. If what you sow is what you reap, what you give is what you get, then think positively and try to sow good things, so that you may be able to reap rich and rewarding harvest. The wand is in your hand. The ball is in your court. Bounce it as you will to.

Chapter 10

BRAHMACHARYA / ABRAHMACHARYA HEALTHY PHASE OF SOUL / INFECTED PHASE OF SOUL

Brahmacharya is a Sanskrit word composed from *Brahma*, the creative force or God and *'charya'* means to be followed, observance or restraint.

Brahmacharya literarily means *acharya* or conduct that leads to realization of *brahman* or one's own self The technical meaning is self restraint, particularly, mastery of self control over sexual pleasure or freedom from lust in thought, word or deed.

Brahma means- the self existent spirit, the absolute reality, the universal self, personal God and the sacred knowledge.

Charya means occupation with engaging, proceeding behaviour; a conduct to follow.

Brahmacharya is commonly translated to mean celibacy for those who are unmarried and fidelity to one partner when married.

Brahmacharya is a mode of behaviour or a virtuous way of life.

Brahmacharya embodies in its meaning an overall lifestyle that helps pursuit the sacred knowledge and spiritual liberation. It is a means and not an end and includes cleanliness, ahimsa, simple living and high thinking, studies, meditation, voluntary restraints on certain diet and intoxicants, and behaviour including sexual behaviour.

Celibacy is one great virtue or *'guna'* of the soul. Every soul strives to attain happiness or joy. This joy can be attained from two sources. It can be from the virtues (*guna*) of the living element *'Guna'* or from non living elements referred to as *'jad'*. When the soul uses the tool of virtues to attain happiness known as celibacy or chastity, it is called *Brahmachaiya*.

Brhama means = *Atma* or soul

Charya = to play

So, playing and engrossing with one's own virtues or simply being in our own true unadulterated nature in the pristine nature of the soul is *Brahmacharya*.

The soul is a master of infinite virtues; hence the pleasure aroused from these virtues is also infinite.

The antonym or opposite of this behaviour is a *Abrahmacharya* or lust.

The 'A' in *Abrahmacharya* denotes 'no'; not to indulge in the virtues of the soul. The domains for enjoyment from *jad* elements virtues or qualities are;

1) Touch
2) Taste
3) smell
4) Form
5) Sound

To strive for happiness from these senses is *Abrahmacharya*. It can be described as the acts of indulging in the pleasures derived from these senses. On the other hand, the celibacy virtue is specified as not craving enjoyment from these 'touch and feel' qualities'.

The enjoyment that can be achieved through these *'jad'*, touch senses can be of many types. It can be pleasures from the possession and wearing of attires, from the soothing effect of wind or cool air on our body, pleasures derived from the relationship with the opposite sex or from female fantasy, etc

And indulging in these is adulterous for the soul and considered as vices or *'doshes'* because the joys from these are temporary and the after effects are disastrous. They are the culprits for causing innumerable births and deaths and they make us rotate in the infinite *sansar*. These are the reasons for the vast suffering and pain in this mundane world.

Knowing the hazardous effects of A*brahmacharya*, now let us contemplate how to overcome such lowly obscene emotions.

One must collect fortitude to overcome these lewd emotions. There are a number of ways to overcome these unchaste emotions and feelings...

Developing a value system and a strong resolute mind will protect us at all times and at all places.

Thinking and analyzing our actions will also be beneficial because it will throw light on the absurdist thoughts.

Say, for instance, a person is attracted towards a woman, lusts for her and wants to have relationship with her but if he can stop for a moment and contemplate that a woman is nothing else but just a bundle of flesh and bones, an object with a series of chemical reactions, a bundle of hormones, biological parts and certain enzymes, would he still be craving for pleasure from mere contact of the flesh or will the thought be so repulsive that it will shake the very foundation of humanity and spirituality? Seers even envisage the body as a basket of waste and poison and if we can imagine the body sans the skin, then the thought of pleasure will turn to one of revulsion, disgust and be loathsome, foul and nauseating.

A woman is analogous to a river having ripples of adoration, amorous enjoyment and sensuality, but if one takes a simple dip in that river, his ascetic mind is disturbed, all his logic goes haywire and he becomes powerless just like the candle, when in contact with fire, loses its originality and becomes a puppet in the hands of fire. It can see itself melting but is helpless. It dissolves and is reduced to nothing but still will stick on to the fire, not realizing that the act is hazardous to its own existence. The same is with us human beings and even before we realize it, all the sensuous acts reduce us to become puppets and prisoners in their hands. It is necessary to rise and unshackle ourselves. The person, who is subdued by the lust or *Raga* of woman, loses the intensity of his pursuit of real fearless happiness; he gets ensnared in the claws of *Raga* and then all his reasoning and sanity is lost.

Think on it. Are we like animals, which do what they feel without any after thoughts? Animals can be exempted because they have no other ways to communicate except touch but as humans, are we more degraded than them? Should we not ponder over our thoughts? The earlier we ponder, the faster the thoughts of lust will disappear from our mind and the lure of the opposite sex will slowly but surely diminish. This tact applies to all other senses too.

Restrain from places that tempt you, move away from groups who inspire you to indulge in these vices.

Even if initially one can't resist the temptations, one can at least physically avoid it and slowly learn to conquer the temptations.

Remember that the characteristics of lust will burn the merits of chastity but if one pines for eternal and unending happiness, then he should spurn the amorous longings and continuously imbibe drugs of the longing for eternal joy or *moksh*. One must keep the fire of longing burning by continuously counteracting on the repugnant thoughts and blowing them away from our minds.

Giving in to lust is like scratching an itch on the body; the more you itch, it becomes more pleasurable and the body asks for more. Pleasures also once indulged will pave a path for more and more; there is no end and no satisfaction. Once you experience it, you will crave for more; the desire for a female is like a poisonous creeper and is the very first sign of distress, but it should be immediately eliminated through the fire of chastity before it gulps down the whole tree i.e. our body on which it grows.

A creeper, as we know, takes the aid of a tree to grow and once it is strong enough, it destroys the tree and lives independently. In the same way, a lustful thought is detrimental to the soul in the long run, so one must be heedful to the first sinful thought otherwise it will lead us to rebirth into the 84 lac nuclei and we will keep oscillating from one birth to another without getting freedom from their bondage.

Diligent people therefore opt for *Brahmacharya* and forsake A*brahmacharya*.

Chapter 11

SADGURU...
THE CONSULTANT OF THE SOUL

What do we mean by *sadguru* or *satguru*?

Satguru means true guru...

Satguru is the title given to an enlightened *Rishi* or *sant* whose life's purpose is to guide his *shishya* along the spiritual path. The summation or end product of this is self realization through realization of God......

What are the qualifications of a *sadguru*?

The first and foremost qualification of the true master or *satguru* is that he must have known the true God Himself. He should have attained realization or *Keval Gyan*.

Scriptures describes *Satguru* as...

He is the real guru who can reveal the form of the formless to the vision of these eyes.

He is the one who teaches the simple way of attaining him through certain religious ways.

Who makes you perceive the supreme spirit whenever the mind attaches itself?

Who teaches you to be still in the midst of all activities?

Ever immersed in bliss, having no fear in mind, he keeps the spirit of universe in the midst of all enjoyments.

Firm as the thunder bolt, the seat of the seeker is established above the void.

He who is within is without. I see him and nobody else.

To sum up, we can say, a *Satguru* is one who develops the good qualities in us, purifies our hearts and sets us on the path of salvation. He fixes our self and carries us beyond the ocean of worldly existence.

THE ROLE OF THE *SATGURU*

The task of a *satguru* is important and exclusive. He is bestowed with the duty of raising the devotee souls from the macabre existence in the form of the ocean of death and birth.

He must lift the souls from the ties and fastens of sublunary objects-*vishay* and passions-*kashay*.

He is a consultant or the physician, the one who recognizes the vices and suggests apt cure.

He frees the diseases or *doshes* and helps to make them less intense.

In the absence of a *satguru*, the *doshes* become manifold and the dire *sansar* becomes multiplied.

The guru preaches ways of liberation. He does not teach the art of acquiring temporal pleasures, but aids to rise above them and achieve the state of *moksh* or sublimity.

The guru must be intelligent, farsighted and philanthropic, to gauge the level of the devotee and guide him according to his caliber.

He should guide the *shravaks* and *shravikas* towards various aspects of *sadharma* like calmness, chastity, courtesy, candour, charity, content, cheer, etc.

He helps through the journey from incompleteness to completeness... from *sansar* to *moksh*.

Guru is the door to happiness...

A guru dispels darkness of ignorance and takes us towards enlightenment.

A guru is a force that understands what is good for our soul much more than we understand ourselves, and it is through guru that we evoke that force to work for us and with us...so the way to eternal bliss is to dedicate spontaneously to guru.

In the presence of a guru, knowledge flourishes, sorrow diminishes, joy swells up without reason...

Along with this spiritual abundance, all talents and potentials manifest more and more.

In every sphere of life, the influence of the guru is visible.

Guru attempts to keep us craving for learning. He helps us grow internally; he helps to reach our spiritual destiny.

Our guru goads us to the path of emancipation... of freedom... freedom from the bondage of births and deaths...

A guru helps us to live all our moments happily... they teach us to live life as it comes any circumstances.

A guru is a beacon to a spiritually aligned life.

He is the one who liberates us from *karmic* infusion.

The guru *shishya* relationship is one of love surrender and faith... you love him, entrust yourself to him, surrender to him and our task is done. HE does the rest...

Through him we get the first glimpse of divinity.

A guru creates, transforms and gives birth to a new *shishya*.

In the presence of a guru, one feels an inward pull, a pull towards one's own existence.

The closer he is to his guru, the more closer he comes with his own self, the more fervently we surrender, the more we experience our freedom.

An understanding and sane person wholly gives himself to his guru, like the small boy in the popular fable. Once, a shopkeeper was pleased with the honesty of a small boy. He showed him a jar of chocolates and asked him to pick up his hands full. The boy quickly contemplated the situation and thought "my hands are small, if I pick up, only a small amount will come to my hands", so he diligently refused and asked the shopkeeper to give him with his own hands knowing that the shopkeeper's hands were larger and he would be entitled to a greater quantity of sweets. In the same way, our capacity to liberate our self is limited but the guru can liberate us faster and quicker.

A guru is a link to that inner divinity with which we are struggling to be in touch with.

It is the philanthropy of the guru that he has made us to know the unknown God, which is the supreme manifestation of our own soul.

The link with guru is born out of experimental reality. The bond between guru and *shishya* does not depend on physical proximity or the number of hours spent in studying his teachings. Once the *shishya* starts implementing the guru's teachings, then he experiences the magic of the sprouting peace and bliss, sheer fulfillment, completeness.

A guru stands on the same pedestal with God; he is the first step on the ladder leading to God.

A guru imbibes faith in us to take the first step even when we are unable to see the whole staircase to *Moksh*. His gratitude is immeasurable.

To end our confusion, we must be in fusion with our guru, to an extent that even when people praise us, or applaud our performance, we should feel that they are praising our guru because everything that we do is endowed by the grace of our guru.

A guru is more than a mere teacher. There are four creators to our life: *Mata, Pita, Guru* and God. *Mata Pita* give us our form, God is formless. The bridge between the form and formless is our *Guru*. He enables us to achieve this natural formless form and hence the relationship between us and the guru is much higher than the physical form alone.

Guru transforms the very chemistry of a person. He can decipher the capacity of a disciple *shishya* and guide him accordingly.

The greatest work of the guru is that he teaches us to be in constant touch with the inner self, he teaches us to be in link with our roots, with our own spirits, with our souls.

The role of a guru is not one; he is sometimes soft like a mother, stern like a father, understanding like a sister, protective like a brother, guider like a guide, illuminator like a philosopher and so much more. He makes it possible for us to take the right path and achieve our goal. He is a true missionary and a perfect seer, a magician who can transform this mundane world into a heavenly abode. He is the captain who takes us from this land of suffering, places us on the beautiful cruise and embarks us on the land of eternal happiness.

There is an averment in a scripture that "Don't taste the nectar if told by *kuguru* and imbibe if commanded by *sadguru*"

When a *neem* tree is nicely poured with water, but it doesn't confer fruits of mango; and the sterile cow is made healthy by nourishing food, but it doesn't give milk. Similarly, *kuguru* cannot confer flowers of *saddharma* or fruits of *moksh*.

Life is not a noun. Life is a verb. It's the guru's attempt for us to keep us learning. Keep living happily in every moment of life. Keep going towards your designed destiny of emancipation.

Guru is presence; a presence that transforms the very chemistry of your being, the greatness of a guru is that he perceives how capable his disciple *shishya* is. He shows a spiritual path which is a science of learning to live in constant touch with center, our own roots, and our spirit in our selves.

A guru takes the responsibility of molding us so that we grow into dignified, worthy and good spiritual being, that we can be a paragon for the next lineage to come.

As we proceed on the pathways of life, we encounter different sets of weather; stormy, smooth, mild and wild. We must keep on reminding ourselves that our guru is in charge of us. He is the controller of our destiny, hence nothing can go wrong.

The *sadguru* is always at the helm, and though storms may blow and thunder may strike, but as our remote control is in his hand, no disaster can occur in our life of any form.

A guru teaches his *shishya*. He says if the umbrella lost its controls, it is going to be destroyed by wind and rain. It will not be of any use to anybody after that. Similarly, our mind too is like that. If you do not hold your mind properly, it will fly away. Unsettled mind is unsteady and unsafe too, it wanders and ultimately gets defiled by the external temporal influences, hence tighten your mind. Hold it properly because tightly held umbrella protects you from the heat and rain. Similarly, properly held mind is not only safe but it also protects you from the unwanted elements which hinder the growth of spirit towards liberation.

The only way to show gratitude towards guru is to live by his messages.

When you are disturbed, with whom do you share your disturbance, makes all the difference. Share it with a person with a lesser maturity, and you will become even more disturbed, and to share it with a person with a higher maturity is to liberate yourself from disturbance. Who has that higher maturity?

SADGURU

Chapter 12

KNOWLEDGE OF BIRTH SPHERES

The Infected Phases of Soul

The spheres of infected - diseased souls to get born are:

There are 84 Lac - nuclei for soul to get born in this universe *sansar*.

1. 7 Lac *pruthvikaya* (living beings with one sense i.e. skin)
2. 7 Lac *apkaya* (living beings with one sense i.e. skin)
3. 7 Lac *teukaya* (living beings with one sense i.e. skin)
4. 7 Lac *vaukaya* (living beings with one sense i.e. skin)
5. 10 Lac *pratyekavanaspatikaya* (living beings with one sense i.e. skin)
6. 14 Lac *sadharanvanaspatikaya* (living beings with one sense i.e. skin)
7. 2 Lac *beindriya* (Two senses: skin and tongue)
8. 2 Lac *teindriya* (Three senses: skin, tongue and nose)
9. 2 Lac *chaurendriya* (Four senses: skin, tongue, nose and eyes)
10. 4 Lac *Devata* (Five senses: skin, tongue, nose, eyes and ears)

11. 4 Lac *Naraki* (Five senses: skin, tongue, nose, eyes and ears)

12. 4 Lac *Tiryanchapancendriya* (Five senses: skin, tongue, nose, eyes and ears)

13. 14 Lac *manushyakaya* (Five senses: skin, tongue, nose, eyes and ears)

Total 84 Lac nuclei

1. *Pruthavikaya* - *'pruthavi'* means earth, *'kaya'* means body, earthly bodies i.e. stones, soils, jewels, metals, salt etc.

2. *Apkaya* - *'ap'* means water, *'kaya'* means body, water bodies i.e. lake water, river, rainfall, ice, hailstone, fog, mist etc

3. *Teukaya* - *'Teu* means fire, *'kaya'* means body, fire bodies i.e. lighting, burning coal, flame, spark, meteor, moving comet, all types of fire, electricity etc.

4. *Vaukaya* - *'vau* means air, *'kaya'* means body; air bodies i.e. all types of air, cyclone, inhalation, whirlwind, wind storm etc.

5. *Pratyeka Vanaspatikaya* - Ten Lac of living beings with independent body are known as *pratyeka vanaspatikaya.*

    'Pratyeka' means personal. *'Vanaspati'* means vegetable. *Kaya* who gets personal body as flora example fruits, flowers, leaves, branches, seeds, trunk, rind, peel or skin. Every form has an independent body and represents a sole living being and all the forms together constitute a tree which has a different soul altogether.

6. *Sadharn Vanaspatikaya* - 14 Lac of living beings with common body for infinite flora. Examples are all types of roots: potatoes, carrot, onion, beat, garlic, mushrooms, tender fruits, aloe vera, moss, spinach.

7. 2 Lac *beindriya* - '*be*' means two and '*indriya*' means senses i.e. these living beings having two senses which are touch and taste.

   Examples: earthworms, conch, stomach insects, leech, flatworm, roundworms, water louse, oyster.

8. 2 Lac *teindriya* - '*te*' means three and '*indriya*' means senses means these living beings having three senses which are touch, taste and smell.

   Examples: ants, louse, black ants, maggot, bedbugs, snail, centipede, termite, *dhamal, korthva,* lungworm, etc.

9. 2 Lac *chaurindriya* - '*chau* means four and '*indriya* means senses means these living beings having four senses which are touch, taste, smell and sight

   Examples: butterfly, mosquitoes, locust, bagai, spider, insect, cricket, grasshopper, honeybees, scorpion, etc.

10. 4 Lac *devata* - '*devata*' who possess five senses i.e. touch, taste, smell, sight and hear. Celestial livings being are known as *devata*.

11. 4 Lac *naraki* - '*naraki*' who possess five senses and the hell inhabitants are known as *naraki* souls.

12. 4 Lac *triyanchapancendriya* - who possess five senses. '*Triyancha*' means animals inhabitants; '*Panchendriya* means five senses. All types of animals who have 5 senses for example the sky birds, the land animals, cow, dog, cat etc.; water inhabitants - fishes, snakes, crocodile etc.

13. 14 Lac *manushyakaya* - *Manushaya* means human beings.

As humans, we are the most developed of all these 84 Lac living beings. We kill innumerable living beings for our happiness out

Savour of the Soul

of ignorance. Now, after knowing our past as these life forms, we should not kill them and feel for them as we feel for our own self.

These all are the infected phases of our own present and past life and if we no more want to rotate in this form, we should remove the infection by a remedy known as "*Dharma* and achieve the healthiest form of soul known as *"Moksh"*.

CHAPTER 13

THE ESSENCE OF HUMAN BIRTH

The highest and noblest objective of human beings is to achieve the innate nature of peace and bliss. All living beings strive to pursue happiness. But the human incarnation is the one and only stepping stone for acquiring happiness. Hence, it is the most longed for, the most coveted for all the 84 lac nuclei of living things. The human being is the most matured nuclei in comparison to all other nuclei. It has been bestowed with the power of the brain, a power unparallel with any other organism. It is the brain that acts as a bridge to connect Hell and Heaven depending on the nature of his deeds and actions. In reality, the true motive behind human birth should be the development of pure *Dharma* and attainment of total detachment i.e. *Moksh,* the beautiful and the final finished end product among all the products in this universe.

A person can succeed in releasing his soul from bondage of *karma* through *dharma* or religious paths and emancipation from *karma* and paves way for the achievement of infinite bliss, infinite knowledge and infinite perception i.e. to the original pristine nature of the pure emancipated soul, and if this herculean task is achieved, then *Atma* becomes *Paramatma* or the supreme soul or God as we call him.

Human birth thus holds the key to opening the doors of this pristine illuminated form of our soul.

Among the 83 lac nuclei that abound the earth, all are not bestowed with all the five senses like humans. The living things, who are bestowed with one, two, three or four senses, are not fit to involve themselves in the process of *dharma* as they don't have the most important tool to understand and perform it—the tool of the brain. Only the living beings with five senses - sight, sound, touch, speech, and taste can strive towards salvation. These beings with five senses can be categorized into four types;

1. Human beings
2. Celestial beings
3. Hell inhabitants
4. Animal incarnations

Even among these...

1) The celestial beings are so engrossed in the happy celestial world and the pleasures of heaven that hardly any of them develop a fascination for the higher bliss of *Moksh*. They do not have the capacity to break the shackles of their *karma* nor are they inclined towards religious salvation. Again, religious restraints like vows, penances, *aradhana*, etc is not possible for them. They cannot take *virti dharma* or renunciation. Hence, *Moksh* is something impossible for them.

2) The inhabitants of hell are so immersed in their sadness, misery and pain that they have no inclination to think and strive about emancipation or freedom from death and life circles. Every moment of hell is like getting death. They are killed again and again and they still regain their bodies so that they can be mercilessly punished for all their ill deeds of their last births, thereby lacking a sole device to help them perform *dharma*. They don't have any seers, gurus or gods to guide them on the right path; hence they are deprived of *Moksh*.

3) Animals, as we all know, have no power of reasoning and understanding, so they are unaware of any ideals or any rituals that would free them from the suffering of this birth and the next. They are deprived of the brain which is the main crux of our religion; hence the *sadhana* of *Moksh* can't be expected from them.

4) Now, that left with only one set of living beings having five senses; the most valuable ones at that: the human beings. The reward of *Moksh* is accessible only by human incarnations. Hence, do we realize how sacred, precious and invaluable our birth is?

Time and again scriptures give instances to prove the preciousness of our human birth and there are so many illustrations that go to prove the rarity of our human birth.

1) Hearth

Say, for example, if an emperor has 34000 countries and 96 crore villages, and if he were to decide that 'I will dine at one house for each meal, just imagine that by the time he finishes one meal with his umpteen villagers, towns and countries, when will the turn of the palace come again? By the time he finishes each house, his life will come to an end. In the same way, if we reflect on our human incarnation, then by the time we finish our births in all living incarnations, we might not be able to get the chance of being born in human form again and again.

2) Dices

Say, a gambler, who is wise, unbeaten, willful and cunning with his dices, throws an open challenge for everyone to come and beat him in the game of dices, alluring each player with a gold coin, can anyone succeed against his wily game? It can still be deemed possible, but once if we fail in the game of one human birth, then note it that another chance to make human life fruitful may be lost forever.

3) Grains

If one accumulates the grains from the whole of *Bharat kshetra* and mixes it with a glass of mustard seeds and then asks an old lady to pick all the mustard seeds and put it back in the glass, will it be possible in the span of her lifetime? Will she ever be successful in her task? It may, by chance, be possible to even pick up all the mustard seeds but it will be impossible to re-track the incarnation of human birth again.

4) Diamond

There was once a *zaveri* who used to deal with invaluable precious stones. Once he had to go to another country for some meeting and when he came back, he came to know that in his absence, his son had made a disastrous deal in diamonds with a foreign trader; he had sold the diamonds at a throw away price. The jeweler got enraged and ordered his son to get back to the trader and trace back the precious stones and not come back till he had accomplished his task.

The son was perplexed. He had no name or address of the trader as he was a stranger to him. Will he be able to retrace the man from the whole world? Will he be able to get back the diamonds that he had sold? Scriptures tell us that it might be possible that the son may sometime come in contact with the trader and the trader may even return his goods but the chances of that were negligible.

Similarly, once you have dealt with the human incarnation and wasted it, it is impossible to achieve it again, so one must make the most use of the given chance.

5) The fulfillment of dream

There was once a small village. Coincidentally, a saint and a landlord lived close to each other.

In the last hours of a night, both coincidentally had a same dream that they had swallowed the whole moon. Both of them rose up immediately after the dream was over.

The saint woke up and informed a *mahant* about the dream. The *mahant* analyzed the dream as a good one and told him that he would get wholesome food with

sweets in offerings on that day, and it turned true; the saint got a full tasty meal and was overwhelmed with that.

On the other hand, the landlord thought that such an auspicious dream should be told to an efficient guru and he did just that. His guru was pleased on hearing his dream and interpreted it by saying, "your good luck will soon strike and you will be a king soon." True to the words of the guru, no sooner had the landlord stepped out of the *upashray* then an elephant poured a *kalash* of *abhishek* on his head and he was declared the king.

He was seated on the elephant and taken to the palace. The saint saw this sight and was jealous. He felt that both of them had the same dream but he gained such a small reward. He wanted to see the same dream again. Would it be possible for him to see the same dream and acquire the same rewards as the landlord? Not really possible as it was impractical and rare. Seers say if his luck would have it, he might be able to visualize the dream once again but if we waste our human birth in lowly things, we will not be entitled to it again. It is a rare gem, so we should use it carefully and frugally.

6) *Radhavedh*

It was the city of Mathura, ruled by King *Jeetshatru*.

He made a declaration-"I will give my daughter's hand only to the one who will win in the art of *Radhavedh*.

All the kings from nearby palaces as well as far off ones came to try their luck.

The task was thus: There was a big vessel filled with steaming hot oil and above the *kadai,* there was a pole with eight planks fitted on its one end and a doll *Radha* was fixed on the fast moving planks. The princes were supposed to hit the black retina of the doll after seeing its reflection in the oil. Would any of them be successful? It was improbable. The same goes with human birth. We have got the human birth with much difficulty but if we fail to materialize it, then the birth goes waste and we don't know when will we be able to access it again.

7) Lather of moss: A huge and deep river has been overlapped with lather of moss. One day, naturally, there was a hole in the lather of moss. A frog moving in water came to the place where there was this hole and through the hole he saw the full moon with its 16 digit. It was spectacular for the frog as he had seen it for the first time in his life. He got a thought of inviting all his siblings, and again he merged in the water to invite them but after coming back again he didn't find the place. How arduous it is to find that place but who do not understand the value of human birth, for them to gain human birth again is most onerous.

8) Yoke: The last gigantic ocean named *swayambhuramana samudra*. In the east of that ocean, we cast the yoke and on the west of the ocean, we cast the needle but due to the waves, accidentally, they both get joint together which is very strenuous, but one who is attached with the mundane pleasure and due to that it merges in 84 Lac nuclei of birth ocean, for them to reward human birth again is not possible.

9) **Atom:** One deity in amusement powdered the wooden pillar and dropped it in a narrow bottle and mounted on the Meru Mountain whose scale was the highest, and casted the fine powder in all directions but to collect the fine powder again and create the wooden pillar again was so laborious. In the same way, once the core of human birth is not apprehending for them, to gain human incarnation again is a tough job.

10) **Gambling:** Once there was a king, to whom his speculator gave a bad news that your son wants to be in your kingdom by killing you. Listening this, the king ponders over 'what to do'. He was perplexed. In this world, every soul plays games to gain position, wealth etc. He found a way out for this. He called his son and told him that to gain our empire, there's one condition. His son asked, "What's the condition?" The king replied by saying that, "in our sovereign there are 108 pillars, who will win without losing a single pillar, will be endowed this kingdom." Due to deity's favour he may win the kingdom but one who has gained the human birth due to *punya karma* and lost it in enjoying sensual objects, for them to gain again is not feasible.

To born in any life from the four inhabitants is the cause for anguish, as due to the control of *Karmic* effect, we get born, and to live life is also in the control of *Karma*, and to get off is also according to *Karmic* effect. As a person is bond with fetters and put into prison, birth is the cause of pain and sorrow. But who procures the human birth from four inhabitants and there he endeavours for his own attributes i.e. right conviction (*Samayak darshan*), right conduct (*Samyak charitra*) and self restraint, then that acquisition of human life is for accolades. The essence of human birth is enlightening of soul, awareness of soul and upliftment of soul.

So, day by day, in every way, we want to become more and more blissful, depurate and spiritual, as putting days into human life is aging but putting life into days is growing. Strive until your last breath to make your every day better than your yesterday and to make your every tomorrow better than your today. Welfare is our human birthright.

Rain fills the size of vessel. Whether our life will be filled with auspicious or inauspicious things depends on the size of our determination and thinking. Our thoughts create our reality. We will get that we focus upon. 'What we focus upon will attract towards our self so focus on to maximum utilization of this human birth as a stepping stone towards spiritual upliftment.

There is nothing in a caterpillar that suggests that it can be a butterfly, yet, it becomes a butterfly. Similarly, though you have wasted your human life until now, your past is not equivalent to your future. What you had been and what you are is inconsequential in what you can be.

Crucify your past and resurrect into a new bright future.

Chapter 14

DHARMA: THE PANACEA REMEDY FOR SOUL

Dharma is a series of steps and one of those last steps, which helps reaching the final destination i.e. *moksh*.

The act of holding the soul from falling down in desperate *sansar* is a trait of *dharma*.

Bearing the soul from degeneration in *sansar* and ascending the soul towards prosperities i.e. emancipation is known as *dharma*.

- In this mundane world, beneficial acts of mind, speech or physique is *dharma*.
- Auspicious thoughts, bona fide speech and beneficent deeds are known as *dharma*.
- The repose imparting element to all living beings in this *sansar* is *dharma*.
- The bond of *punyanubandhipunyakarma* with the soul is *dharma*.
- The device which is the root cause of all prosperity, upliftment of the soul and mainspring of emancipation is *dharma*.

- The causes for succession of *punyanubandhipuny* karma and *sakam nirjara-* the detachment of *karma* from the spirit is *dharma*.

- The beneficial and happiness endowing non-violence is *dharma*

- To abandon selfishness and to accept the act of philanthropy is *dharma*.

- Magnanimous, beneficent and generous conduct is *dharma*.

- Five codes of conduct *Gyana-Achar, Darshana-Achar, Charitra- Achar, Taap-Achar and Virya-Achar* are known as dharma.

  - *Gyan-Achar - Gyan* means knowledge and *achar* means act.

  - *Gyana-Achar* means to be prompt to acquisitive *gyan* and to confer altruistic *gyan* to aspirant souls.

  - *Darshan-Achara* means to be prompt to have reverence for icon of God.

  - *Charitra-Achara* 'means to flow the religious rites of *samiti* and towards seeker souls.

  - *Tapa-Achara* means always prompt to perform different types of *Taap* as per an individual's potential.

  - *Virya-Achara* means never conceal ones strengths and power in an individual's.

- Right tenets, right knowledge and right code of conduct is called *dharma*.

- Awareness of the soul is *dharma*.

- The inclination to move towards spirituality is *dharma*.

- The innate sacred inclination of the soul is *dharma*.

- The absence of passion *khasay* is *dharma*.

- Alms *Dana*, celibacy *Shil*, penance *Taap* and auspicious propensity *Bhav* is *dharma*.

- For any living being, any act which is beneficial to soul in present is *dharma* for that living being.

- Propitious auspicious inclination is *dharma*.

- *Dharma* is the only sole device which from the roots extinguishes incontrollable and uncountable passions of creatures.

- The only element which has the strength to desist the anguish of all creatures in this mundane world is *dharma*.

- *Dharma* is a veritable nectar, *Dharma* awards glee and serenity at the time of death, it bestows the abatement of passion and coolness, and *Dharma* is a sole comrade which follows the soul in the next incarnations also.

- *Dharma* is a purgative drug to purify our soul from smudge of *karma*.

- *Dharma* is the highest rapture (Happiness).

- *Dharma* bestows heaven and emancipation.

- *Dharma* is the road for crossing the wild *sansara*.

- *Dharma* imparts very fine qualities like a Guru.

- *Dharma* is a heat for the destruction of defilement of *karmic* body.

- Auspicious thoughts are cause for *punya-karma*

- Evil thoughts are cause for *paap-karma* known as *adharma*.

- *Dharma* is a mansion of bliss.

- *Dharma* is a ship for crossing the ocean of disasters.

- *Dharma* is a bail for the acquisitions of the wealth of complete glee.

- *Dharma* is moonlight to dispel the darkness of wrong belief.

- *Dharma* is a bridge for boundless ocean of existence which is hard to cross like the sea.

- *Dharma* is a wishing tree in the desert of sansar.

- *Dharma* is an ocean of nectar of suitable thought and pleasant speech by the complete renunciation of falsehood.

- *Dharma* is the beacon for overcoming an ocean of existence.

- *Dharma* is a purifying agent for the defilement of karmic body.

- *Dharma* is a ship for wandering in the ocean of sansar filled with a whirlpool of numerous birth nuclei.

- *Dharma* is a salubrious lotion for those who are infected with the various passions in this mundane world.

- *Dharma* is the search light in the dense jungle (wood) of sansar.

- *Dharma* is like powder of alum which is successful in the task of purifying the mind analogy to water of souls who are apt for emancipation.

Without knowing *dharma* we cannot perform *dharma dhyan* (meditation) and without *dharma dhyan* there is no equanimity (*samata*), without equanimity there is no *sukla-dhyan* (meditation), without *sukla-dhyan* there is no *vitragata*, without *vitragata* there is no *keval-gyan* (omniscience), w i t h o u t omniscience there is no *moksh*. Hence one has to first and foremost acknowledge *dharma* to reach the target of sheer happiness (*moksh*)

It is certain that the fruits of *dharma* are being perceptible by self-realization in present which are a composed state of mind and the fruits in the next incarnations are many more i.e. *Satgati* and *moksh*

In this mundane there is not a sole substance which can bestow instant fruits which *dharma* can confer, hence the strength of *dharma* in comparison to all other strengths is incomparable, unparallel and unique.

To release the spirit from sins is the main significant characteristic of *dharma*. As sins are paramount causes for anguishes.

Any activities which desist the passions of souls is *dharma*.

The command of Tirthankar Parmatma (God) is Dharma

When we are deeply connected with *dharma*, we feel that our inner-self gets purified from *karma*. In our thoughts, in our feelings and in our conscious, we fill calm. Every substance has its own pristine nature.

Here fire has the pristine nature to impart warmness.

Fresh breeze has the pristine nature to impart refreshment.

Water has the pristine nature to impart-coolness, quench thirst and sanitation.

Garden has the pristine nature to impart aroma.

Staying close to fire keeps us warm. By walking through fresh breeze we feel refreshed. By being in running water, we feel clean and cool.

Savour of the Soul

Stay long enough in a rose garden and we start smelling like a rose. So, we inherit the traits of what we are connected to.

Similarly, *dharma* too has its own pristine nature to impart "happiness" who accepts it.

Chapter 15

FORGIVENESS-KSHAMAPNA
THE HEALTHY PHASE OF THE SOUL

Forgiveness is the virtue of the soul, the opposite of anger. To forgive is to set a prisoner free and discover that the prisoner was you!

The word 'forgive' means to wipe the slate, to pardon or to pay a debt. When we wrong someone, we seek his or her forgiveness in order to restore the relationship. It is an act of love, mercy and grace.

Psychologists generally define forgiveness as a conscious and deliberate decision to release feelings of resentment or vengeance towards a person or group who has harmed you, regardless of whether they actually deserve your forgiveness.

Forgiveness is that fragrance that the flower sheds on the heel that crushes it. Forgiveness is letting go of the past and is therefore the means of correcting our misconceptions. Forgiveness is like this: a room can be dark because you have closed the curtains and the doors but the sun is shining outside and the air is fresh. In order to get that fresh air, you have to get up, open the window, and draw the curtains apart.

Traits and characteristics of forgiveness

- The weak can never forgive. Forgiveness is the attribute of the strong.
- To err is human, to forgive is divine.

- The forgiver has a bright and happy future.
- A happy relationship results from the union of two forgivers.
- Forgiveness is the economy of the heart.
- Forgiveness is the sweetest domain of peace.
- To forgive is the highest and the most beautiful form of love.
- Forgiveness is the economy of the heart. Forgiveness saves the expenses of anger and hate, the cost of composed state of mind, the waste of spirits.
- Forgiveness can cure many mental and physical illness, its healing power is astounding.
- To unburden yourself of your past, first and foremost embrace forgiveness.
- Forgiveness is the gift of an adamantine heart.
- Forgiveness is a prudent virtue of the soul.
- Forgiveness means strength.
- Forgiveness is the root of all virtues.
- Forgiveness means freedom from all ties and opening of all ties.
- The word *kshama*: 'ksha' means a knot and 'ma' means to destroy.

Today all relationships are caught up in a number of knots -the knots of a difference of opinion between a father and a son, between a guru and his disciple, the knot of misunderstanding between a husband and wife, the knots of inaccessible jibes between a master and his servant.

- Violence is the strength of the wicked

    Penalty is the strength of the kings.

Service is the strength of women.

And forgiveness is the strength of the virtuous.

- We must develop the capacity to forgive. He who is devoid of the power to forgive is devoid of the capacity to love.
- If one says I can forgive but cannot forget, then he means he cannot forgive. Forgiveness is like a cancelled and torn cheque which cannot be used again.
- There is some good and some bad in all of us. If we accept this then we are less prone to hate our enemies.
- The stupid never forgive nor do they forget. The wise forgive but do not forget.
- We are all full of weaknesses and flaws. Let us mutually pardon each other of our follies.
- Forgiveness is the art of liberating oneself.
- It is like liberating ourselves from the heavy baggage of hate.
- Between the hater and the hatred, it is the hater who gets hurt more. Thus, forgiveness is not liberating the other from you. It is the tact of liberating yourself from the others.
- Forgiveness is giving up the right to hurt others for hurting you.
- It is the act of bestowing peace to oneself and all around.
- Forgiveness is to endure, to let go other's repugnant and vile acts. It is the refrigerating agent for us as it projects the soul against the heat of the faults of others.
- A little pain in one part of the body should not stop the functioning of the whole body. Something that has gone wrong in a certain phase of your life should not halt the

progress of your life. Imagine yourself holding a chair in the air. Though the weight of the chair is the same, the longer you lift the chair, the heavier the chair will seem to be. Carrying is an effort, dropping is a relaxation. You have been labouring with your past. Make a decision and relax. It will relieve you.

The best example of forgiveness:

In the Mahabharata, we have read that, after the victory of the *Pandavas, Aswathama* came at midnight and killed five of *Draupadi's* sons. The ocean of victory turned into a sea of lamentation. The shock sent *Draupadi* into fits of unconsciousness. *Bhima* and *Arjun* ran after *Aswathama*, arrested him and brought him before *Draupadi*.

Shri Krishna said, "He is the killer of your son. What punishment would you like to award for such a heinous crime? A single blow from *Bhima* will break his head and remove it from his trunk."

Draupadi burst into tears. The gruesome murder of her sons filled her heart with pain. She sobbed, "I am feeling so terrible about the loss of my sons. I don't want his mother to experience the same pain. Don't kill him. I am experiencing the agonizing pain of separation. Let not his mother experience it."

And *Ashwathama,* the murderer, was released. This is the grandeur of forgiveness. The *puranas* describe vengeance as the gateway to hell. Quran titles it as the Satan's son. The Bible compares anger and revenge as the burning volcano as it burns a man to ashes.

The greatness and advantages of forgiveness

The practice of forgiveness is one most important contribution to the healing of the world. Forgiveness is the key to the action of freedom. Forgiveness gives the forgiver a peace of mind and protects him from corrosive anger. It involves in the letting off of negative emotions. Forgiveness makes us happy. It can make other people happy too.

Forgiveness improves our health. When we dwell on grudges, our blood pressure and pulse rate spikes, showing signs of stress and it also damages our body. Forgiveness lowers our stress levels. Forgiveness strengthens the immune system and makes us more resistant to illness.

Forgiveness sustains relationships. It repairs relationships before they dissolve. Forgiveness boosts kindness and connectedness. Forgiveness is the path to 'true enduring peace!'

Chapter 16

MICHAMMI DUKKADAM

The Healthy Phase of the Soul

The *Tirthankar Parmatmas,* the enlightened souls, the supreme philanthropists highlighted the fact that "our *'Sukruts'* or good deeds are the primary reason for the perennial happiness of our soul and in the same way our *'Dushkruts'* pave the way for our pain and suffering and as a consequence, it leads to the forlorn state of the soul."

From eternal time, the strong delusive *"Mithyatva Mohaniya karma* pollute and impure the soul with vices or *"Kashay* like *Raga, Dvesh,* Conceit, Avarice, Envy, Jealousy etc. These vices completely overpower and mislead the soul, obstructing right knowledge and right conduct too.

The solution to the problem lies in the magical word *"MICHAMMI DUKKADDAM'.*

What does this magical term mean and why should it be practiced?

Well in short, it is an admission of our own faults and a resolution to refrain from it. When we hurt others with our actions, we should say *'MICHHAMI DUKKADAM'* i.e. "I agree that I was wrong and I am sorry for the pain it has caused!"

Unless and until we are not perturbed by our faults and are not inclined towards gaining virtues or *guna,* we will not be able to erase these faults *dosh* and if this is so, we will not be able to impart *Michammi Dukkadam* in the true sense of the word.

There is no bigger sin than maintaining the friendship with wrong tenets or vices, and there is no better friend than the one who will guide us towards recognizing our own foes and helps us to find our *dosh.*

The reciting of the word *Michammi Dukkadam* with the awareness of the deep inclination of its meaning related to one of the highest commandments of our *Paramatmas* is included in our religious rites and aims at negating sins *dosh* and giving *Michammi Dukkadam* for that.

Secondly, by chanting "*Michammi Dukkadam*" the inclination (*parinama*) of the aspirant becomes more '*Samvegshil*' that means analyzing the intensity with which these *dosh* had been performed and developing a deep disgust towards these faults with the same intensity with which they had been performed. This intense disgust is known as *Samveg Parinama.*

Thirdly, by reciting the word *Michammi Dukkadam,* we take a resolution of refraining ourselves from indulging in those *dosh* again and this is another magical word which will ward off a lot of *karma* resulting in '*Nirjara*'.

HOW DOES THIS MAGNANIMENT *NIRJARA* HAPPEN?

Nirjara is the partial oozing out of *karma* or the partial eradication of *karma* from our soul. This eradication or detachment of the soul from the *karmas* is called Nirjara and is therefore synonymous with *Michammi dukkadam.* The ratio of the intensity of Nirjara is directly related to the intensity with which *Michammi Dukkadam* is given and vice versa.

The meaning of every alphabet of *Michammi Dukkadam* and the etymology meaning of *Michammi Dukkadam* is as:

1. MI : *mrudu* and *mardava*
2. CHHA : to desist faults
3. MI : to be abstinent (self restraint) *virati*
4. DU : to condemn oneself
5. KKA : I have done sinful acts
6. DAM : transgressing sins by abatement devices

1. MI: *mrudu* and *mardava, mrudu* means softness and *mardava* means to relent.

   Mrudu means stopping the physique and *mardava* means the inclination towards relenting. The voluntary acknowledgement of our *dosh* is not possible if we are indulgent in arrogant propensity.

2. *CHHA:* When we recite the word *Michammi Dukkadam*, we mentally ensure ourselves that we will not perform the same *dosh* again. This deep profound resistance is the meaning of *chha*.

3. MI: I am in a stage of pledge, on a platform of self-restraint.

   This means when we are conferring *Michammi Dukkadam*, at that time we should be in *charitra* (in pledge). Only then this word works out.

4. DU: I have developed an aversion towards my own *Dosh* filled soul. This means that I had willingly performed the *dosh*, indulged in them and relished them. I am now very ashamed and remorseful of the act and have developed an aversion towards the *dosh*. I am neutralizing my soul. I am purifying my soul from vices or "*Ashubha Karma*".

5. KKA: These sins had been performed by me and no one else. This states that I have committed a lot of sins in the past but we never labeled them as sins. The act of acknowledging these acts as sinful acts is known as KKA; the act of shriving or confessing these *dosh* to *"satguru* exactly in the same way as they had been performed without any inhibition and fear, paves the way to immaculate the souls.

6. DAM: Transgressing *dosh* by abatement means the exact antonym of *dosh*, inclination is abatement. By doing this, the *dosh* gets vandalized and the soul gets purged of the sins.

   Michammi Dukkadam thus literally means "purgation of the soul" i.e.: Whenever I perform sinful acts or develop hatred, jealousy etc, these acts impure my own soul, it blemishes my own soul and tarnishes it.

   But the wonderful act of *Michammi Dukkadam* i.e forgiveness, acceptance and repentance along with a firm resolution to restrict from this acts in future; which cleanses, purifies and illuminates our soul and makes it blemish free.

   This is the essence, it is the crux of our great festival 'the *Paryushan Parva*', the eight day festival where we perform regression for all the sinful and bashful acts performed knowingly or unknowingly during the phase of the whole year.

   The last day of the festival and the most important day is for the clearance of all ill feelings; all sinful thinking of the mind, word and body asking for forgiveness before the final rites which is '*Samvatsari pratikraman.*'

   The '*pratikraman*' is another wonderful ritual. It literally means moving back or retreating from our *dosh*.

   '*Pratt*' means back; '*kramman*' means to come.

Therefore, in short, to come back into our innate self and our own true nature of virtuousness, along with the magnanimity of forgiving and forgetting the sins performed by us, and also by others, are the true rites of *pratikraman*.

Without recognizing and repenting our *dosh,* our demerits, the *Michammi Dukkadam* imparted by us will be void and ineffective and just keep us sailing in the sea of *'sansar'*...

The journey of our *sansar,* the to and fro sail from births to deaths will end when we develop an aversion towards our *dosh* and encourage a penchant feeling or a deep inclination towards our *guna* or virtues. This is the beginning of the journey towards the real nature of our soul.

Chapter 17

INTROSPECTION-ATMANIRIKSHANA-MIRROR FOR THE SOUL

Healthy Phase of the Soul

We are under our own surveillance even if we are not being seen from the left or right, front or back, up or down but still, when we behold our self or our conscience it is known as introspection *atmanirikshana*.

Atmanirikshana is made of two words *'atma'* which means soul and *'nirikshana'* that means to visualize or to see very minutely. To see our own self very minutely is *atmanirikshana*.

The mirror presents slime on the physique; the introspection is analogous to the mirror for presenting slime on the soul. The slime on the soul is a fault formation. If our vision is without predilection for our own selves, then obviously it will present the soul virtues and faults as it is. This too is known as introspection.

Introspection engenders awareness which doesn't settle us but keeps changing us virtually, doesn't settle but keeps growing higher, doesn't despair but keeps spurring, and doesn't remain sordid but depurate us perpetually. These are the qualities of introspection.

It is to observe the life cassette, to retrospect the life cassette. Cease as and when the squalid is being observed as the squalid has

Savour of the Soul

various folds like illusion, ignorance, ego, envy, lust, rudeness, rage, deceit, avarice, attachment and many more.

After beholding it minutely, contemplate on each fault, measure the intensities, confess to *sadguru*, choose the appropriate detergent agent for the squalid, relate with the soul, perform atonement, penance and expiate for it, observe the aftermath, that the adornment of virtues gets embossed which is the beauty of the soul, trait of soul, and innate nature of the soul.

Introspection is self discovery and in the journey of introspect and retrospect we discover what we are now, were in past, and what we are capable of in the future.

The water at the seashore looks so still and pure until the stone is not thrown but when thrown, the consequence is that the impurities appears on the surface of the water. The fact is that the water was not pure. This analogues to the soul, prima facie when we look at our self everything looks sedate but when it is observed without predilection, or some adverse situation occurs or when we ponder over something, then the proclivity is manifested and smudge of manifold is being visualized i.e. wrong tenets, passion, immaturity, low esteem, lust and selfish yearns.

Introspecting daily makes our inner voice very lucid and strong. It will make us grow more in awareness which is a way to purify the soul. We can judge ourselves where we are standing. We can grow our self by appreciation as it is a unique remedy to scale higher and self criticism is cleansing and purifying the soul from the scum of faults due to bond of *karma*.

Due to introspection, we will discover a guru within us. One of the greatest gifts to mankind is gift of self awareness. Man alone can analyze his own experiences and improve; man alone not only studies a subject, but also becomes the subject of his own study. Self awareness must be nurtured and developed, but how? By daily practicing introspection at the close of everyday before going to sleep, practice a mental run of all our experiences of that day. Recalling each one of them, you will discover through introspection that where your fault formation is.

Due to the lack of introspection how often do we know 'what to do' before the incident, we also know 'what we should have done' after the incident and yet, our own knowledge betrays us during the incidents. We have solutions to all the problems of the world and yet, we aren't able to solve our own problems, why? Due to lack of introspection, in fact there is obsessive accumulation of knowledge, but there is dearth of true knowledge. In this mundane, the nearest to us is our own self and the farthest is the star but the irony is that we have gathered complete knowledge of the farthest stars and a great ignorance of one's own self, though we are the nearest to us.

Step back and observe. A painter, after every few strokes, takes a step back and observes his own painting. That's how he understands whether further strokes have to be. That's what introspection is all about; stepping back and observing our own life and developing the life's painting more and more accurately and beautifully that it becomes paragon for others to reach.

I will analyze my experiences and improve myself by standing apart from myself and practice introspection at the dawn and close of everyday.

Questions about the past are what introspection is. Introspection is not just about recollecting events mechanically, but critically examining them with the right kind of questions. How better could we have responded to the situation is an introspective question. It helps to train the mind to think in a constructive Maaner and to respond more effectively in the future.

One of the most useful introspective questions is to ask ourselves that what were those moments during the day when we acted with 'unawareness', 'without pondering' or 'ignorance', without questioning and enquiring our mind. It will not be possible to free ourselves of the vast amount of ignorance that surrounds our lives as it is a door to agonies.

Ignorance is the root cause of our ineffective responses to life situations, and questions are the way out.

Introspection and retrospection beget awakening.

The beginning is from where you begin. Begin today. Begin now. The person you will become in life is waiting for you in future. You must go and meet him. So, focus your energies in being an architect of your life. We converse metaphorically.

Think of a notebook with several pages. Each page in itself is just an open page. It is up to us to either scribble on it or write true concepts on it which benefits us, cut short our agonies. Irrespective of whether we scribble on it or pen ethics on it, we can still turn to the next page and again have the choice of either scribbling on it or writing beneficial concepts. Till the notebook ends, the freedom of choice to use or abuse the pages of the notebook can be akin to our life and each open page in it is a new day in our life. The dawn of fresh new day offers us the choice of using or abusing the day. Till we embrace life, the freedom of choice to use or abuse the day of our life purely rests with us. Whatever be our age, as a worst case scenario, even if we have wasted the entire past of our life, we can still make a new beginning. We can make the most of each day of our life from now on and create a life that can be cherished.

The rear view mirror of a car can aid in driving, but we have to look ahead through the windshield, for that's the only way to reach our destination. Your past serves as a rear view mirror reflecting our accomplishments and our failures. It teaches you the lessons on what to do and what to drop for our own benefit and welfare. We must mature out of our past and meet the future head on. With derived maturity from our past, we must and we can do much more with our future. Our past has left us a long time back, so what is the point in continuing to carry it on our head. We can help a person caught in the jaws of a crocodile, but how do we help a person who thinks he is caught in the jaws of a crocodile while all he has is just the picture of the crocodile under his feet? Nothing is a greater retardant to growth than the burden of emotions of the past. The trouble with the emotions of the past is that it leaves us with scratched spectacles and we become incapable of seeing life as it is. Someone misbehaved with us in the past and because of those scratched spectacles, every new acquaintance and friend too appears to be a rogue.

Treat your past not as a source of hurt and agonies, but as an experience that you needed to gain the maturity.

The process of chiseling may not have been pleasant but without it we won't be the sculpture we are today. Use our today to contact our future, and not to dissect our past.

The past of an exquisite sculpture was a stone, which took numerous blows from the chisel of a sculptor.

The past of a flute in the hands of a maestro was a bamboo that was seasoned in fire and with holes drilled into it with hot iron rods.

A glittering diamond was once an unnoticed piece of carbon.

We too can go through anything in life, but we can become what we want to become in life, if we crucify our erroneous past and resurrect into a new future. Introspection converts into awakening and awakening into spur of the soul.

More instances of results of awakening:

Our driver didn't turn up yesterday. When we ask him the reason he says, "last night, I drank too much and in the hangover I slept a little extra." Will we continue to keep him with us? Or will we sack him?

Our accountant has done some adjustments in our company's accounts and misappropriated some money. Do we keep him or will we immediately sack him from the organization?

We noticed our housemaid taking 500 rupees from our shirt pocket. When we enquire about it, she blatantly denies. We all will say that she is lying. Will we engage her anymore? Or will we sack her?

Our gardener turns back after two days and says, "I got involved with another woman and that became an issue with my wife. I have to sort things out and that's why I could not make it the last two days."

After hearing this, will we continue with him or sack him?

That means we will not tolerate the driver having habit of drinking, accountant who is cheating, housemaid who is lying, etc. That means that we will not tolerate any blemish in the character of others. Then, what about us? Why is our character expectation always higher from others than the character expectations from our own self?

Hence, be aware of one's own self

Everything about our life too should change in those moments. Our character expectation from our self, our behaviour, our thoughts and everything about us should redefine in those moments.

How we smell depends on what we stand next to - a rose, a garden or a drain. We should begin feeling the fragrance of that inner change by holding these 'life redefined moments' very close to our heart. As there is no difference between the human being and another human being as long as the potential is sleeping within. The difference between a legend and an also-ran is the difference in the manifestation of the latent potential within them. Every human being has within him the autobiography. Every history reader, every ethic reader can be a history and ethics maker.

In every seed is the promise of a thousand forests. In every moment of life is hidden a promise that can make an *atma*, *parmatama* and that *parmatama* or god becomes paragon for thousands to uplift themselves spiritually.

Every moment has in it the seeds to author a supreme soul and acme happiness. The soul who demonstrates intense awareness to that moment of life has authored a new future for itself.

There is a hidden meaning in every moment of life. Let us live life with intense awareness to unravel this meaning. Wait in faith... our moment is just coming.

After introspection, contemplation with self:

- My real self is pure conscious, which possesses infinite vision, knowledge, power and bliss, and is free of all attachment *raga* and aversions *dvesh*.

- The ultimate goal of life is happiness and that can be possible by releasing oneself from the bond of *karma,* which means total freedom from all attachment and aversion which is known as 'emancipation' or freedom of soul from eternal pain.

- I wish to treat each and every soul as my own self.

- I shall have amity for every soul, compassion for physically and mentally agonized souls, have indifferent inclination for faulty souls and cheeriness for virtuous souls.

- I wish to follow the path of emancipation, which is right conviction, right knowledge and right conduct.

- I wish to perform atonement for wrong conviction, for wrong knowledge and wrong conduct, which is an inner bath for smudged souls by confessing to *sadguru* as they are only compassionate consultants, who are masters to negate and nullify the soul from diseases of faults.

Chapter 18

GRATITUDE OR *KRUTAGNATA*

Gratitude is the healthiest of all human emotions. The more you express gratitude, the more you get.

Gratitude is the finest blossom which springs from the soul.

A grateful mind is a great mind which eventually attracts itself to great things.

Gratitude is an emotion expressing gratefulness and appreciation for what one has. By cultivating the habit of gratitude, we can increase our well being and happiness.

Gratefulness, and its expression to others, is associated with inverted energy and optimism.

The literal meaning of Gratitude:

Gratitude is that merit of the soul known as *'krutagnata'*. There is no attitude like gratitude. A heart laden with gratitude need not search for spiritual abundance. Instead, spiritual abundance will flow into your life naturally. It can be defined as the quality of being thankful. The readiness to show appreciation for and to return kindness for all the small acts rendered to us that has made us happy, contented & joyful.

Gratefulness is the charming gardener which makes the souls blossom. It is respect to the giver. But who is the universal giver, one may ask.

God and the Guru are the ultimate givers in this universe and thereby hold the first stand as regards supreme gratitude. They have endowed in us the sheer sermons, consequent of their supreme knowledge or *keval gyan*. *Keval gyan* is the aftermath and reward of many fold *sadhanas* from previous incarnations in which they strived hard to do *sadhana* and after achieving their goal, have been magnanimous to confer it to us too, and have always guided us on the same path. They recurrently try to articulate and confer wisdom about the distorted, temporal, maimed, selfish, and veritable nature of dire *sansar* or the mortal illusionary world.

God is the supreme guru. He has passed the ocean of knowledge to their disciples, made them competent to continue the process of showering knowledge down to their lineage, in succession to their genealogy; these sermons have reached to us. This is the supreme gratitude of the supreme gurus, means god, on apt creatures.

The most apt way to elaborate and return this gratitude is by creating spiritual abundance. Our thoughts create our reality and we get what we deserve. We can become abundant-minded by being grateful for what we have and for engendering our own potentials.

One may ask, "How can I be so grateful when so much in my life is going wrong?" Well, you have all the more reason to be grateful, for it is only gratitude that's going to set our life in the right direction.

Be grateful for the difficult times, for they helped us to become more mature.

Be grateful for the obstacles encountered, for they developed your character's strength.

Be grateful for your mistakes, for they taught you lessons. Be grateful for your limitations, for they helped you develop and evolve.

Be grateful for those who betrayed you, they helped you to become independent.

A pinch of gratitude added to all our experiences is the right approach to be happy. All our happy moments are due to the sprinkle of gratitude that we have intentionally or unintentionally added to all the moments of our life. This is the recipe to prove that our lives are beautiful.

When we forget to sprinkle this salt of gratitude, we feel incomplete, irritated, depressed, shallow and unhappy. The small pinch makes the experience complete, irrespective of the actual outcome. The act of gratitude gives us a liberated feeling.

Again, when we do something with gratitude, we don't expect anything in return. Our actions become selfless and things done with selfless motive always have a miraculous outcome.

To conclude, let us practice the virtues of gratitude and unlock the fullness in our life. This virtue turns what we have in life into enough and more. It turns denial or refusal into acceptance, chaos into order, confusion into clarity, a meal into a feast, a house into a home, and a stranger into a friend. This feeling gives rise to constant awakening, leading to new unbelievable wonders.

The important and key point in this is that experiencing and expressing gratitude is an important part of any spiritual practice. It opens the heart of active and positive emotions centered in the brain. The positive emotions can soothe distress and broaden the thinking patterns, so we can develop larger and more expansive view of our lives.

Chapter 19

ATTITUDE-OUR OUTLOOK OF LIFE- OUR MENTAL SPECTACLES

ATTITUDE IS THE MENTAL SPECTACLE WITH WHICH WE VIEW LIFE

If the spectacles are crystal clear and beautiful, the world appears beautiful but if the spectacles are misty, spotted or stained, then the world seems nasty!

If we wear the specs upside down then the world will look topsy-turvy.

Who is to be blamed, the world or the specs? It is our attitude.

Hence, if our attitude is right, we will be able to make our life right and vice versa.

Let us ponder over the meaning of attitude and what does it stand for? What do we mean by the term attitude? It is important to understand this before we move forward towards right and wrong attitude, good or bad attitude and of course positive and negative attitude.

Attitude is nothing but habitual thoughts and our approach to life. Repeated actions become habit and repeated thoughts frame our attitude.

Now, having deciphered the meaning of attitude, let us evaluate the consequences of good and bad attitude. Let us remember that positive attitude is neither a sure guarantee for success nor does negative attitude guarantee failure.

Let us weigh the pros and cons.

Having positive attitude relates to paving ways for how things can be done rather than insisting that it can't be done. It looks at ways to cross obstacles and achieve tasks but negative attitude focuses on excuses. Not for doing but on creating barriers, so that it need not be done. All the failure and disabilities in life are the consequences of wrong attitude and the poorness of attitude becomes poorness of character.

So, always maintain a positive attitude. It is not necessary to create new horizons but to view the existing horizons with the right spectacle. It is a fact that we cannot change fate but it is possible to change our mental attitude, our approach, and our mindset towards life.

Nothing can stop a man with the right attitude to achieve his goals as his outlook perceives things that are genuinely in his benefit whatever the situation may be and however complicated things may be, the right attitude always penetrates through the situation and pulls out the quintessence of compose.

In sharp contrast, nothing in the world can aid the man with a negative attitude, however, good or right the situation maybe, his wrong mental attitude will never be able to decipher the right and the wrong, the advantages and the disadvantages, but right attitude is the fantastic art of living, which enables and ensures a peaceful, blissful and joyful life.

It is a well known fact that life is 10% of what happens and 90% of how we react to it, if we want peaceful repercussions; always evaluate the consequences in a positive way, in a beneficial way. The circumstances merely depend on how we react towards it. Hence our mode of reaction is the prime source of peace, purge and perfection...

What we sow, we reap, what we bestow, we yield. It is sane to acknowledge or blame the consequences of our past *karma*, on the contrary, if we do not take it positively, new *karmic* matters are further infused on the soul and the aftermath is more appalling and thus a more horrible *sansar*.

If you envisage a fantastic beneficial vision for tomorrow, you will find power and purpose in your work today, thus for this you must envisage a scenic tomorrow.

We often hear people say, "We are saturated with life" or "my life has come to a standstill", but have you ever pondered over the truth behind this? In reality, there is no such thing such as a saturated with life; it is just a saturation of thoughts and in reality there is no stagnation of life; it is just a stagnation of people. Life is like an open parenthesis, just open and fill it as much as you want, as there is no closed parenthesis.

There is as much room as your heart can conceive and as much room as your mind can believe. The only perfect definition of life is more, more and more; there is always room for more but, of course, it should be in the positive, must be beneficial, and it must be the outcome of true perception of *samyakdarshan* or ultimate knowledge.

Life gives many examples of maintaining the positive attitude.

"Mummy, I have taken the cough syrup on my own," said the little girl proudly.

"Did you shake it well?" The mother asked.

She nodded but added, *"Mumma,* why do you ask the same question again and again?"

The mother patiently replied, "Because it is very important to shake the bottle before consuming or else the important ingredients will remain at the bottom and you will not benefit from the drug, so you need to shake it properly and mix it well before taking it." All of you must have seen the instruction on bottles that advise to shake well before use.

The same applies to life too. Sometimes, when we retrospect our life, we realize that it has not taken the shape as we wanted it to be. We then go through turmoil, turbulence in life but when this happens we must feel shaken up and be happy rather than crying over it. After all, someone is shaking our life and helping us to evaluate life. If shaken well, it can bring out every potentiality, every possibility and everything that can be of value to us, enabling us to bring it to the surface, so that we can utilize it to our benefit. Remember, if we do not regularly shake up our lives, we may end up living a shallow life, a life devoid of all our capacities, all our potentials, all our talents, all the residue of great possibilities that could have been feasible will settle down unused and unknown like the unshaken liquids in the bottles but when we shake up, a new and better quality may crop up which has laid dormant at the bottom. Testing time always reveals a new aspect, a new talent, a new capacity that we have been unaware of, the ordeals and the trials of our life, are our shakers.

So, whenever we feel shaken up in life, we should close our eyes in gratitude and thank the mental attitude and ask ourselves, "Why has it been a bad day?" Evaluate with a positive outlook and your intelligence will give you umpteen reasons and offer you options to cope up with it. It will manage to give you answers to life's most challenging questions to difficult situations. If your attitude is positive, you can even be an advocate for devil in you for the negativity in you, for the bad in yourself and you'll be able to give positive reasons against that thinking. You will be able to argue, give reasons, formulate verdicts and offer a positive aspect to the negative thoughts to negative feelings and to wrong assumptions. You will be able to smoothly guide the bad notions towards the good, the right and positive directions. If you think about troubles, your mind will hunt for more troubles and will give you a stock of troubles. It will pressurize you with difficulties and will burden you with negativity but just slide away to solutions; you will feel your mind is real solution finder, a real relief giver and a peace provider.

All this goes on to prove a positive attitude, a positive approach, a positive outlook, a positive thought and can be a stepping stone to success to achieve the impossible. It can be a spirit charger and it works wonders with the mind and with life and gives new meaning to life. It widens your visions, illuminates your soul, liberates it from the shackles of negated thoughts and works towards the ultimate goal, that of a joyful, a liberated, a blissful, a satiated state of the soul, the *sahajananddasha,* the enlightened and sublimated phase of life.

Chapter 20

DIKSHA - RENUNCIATION

Diksha means renunciation. Renouncing the world and walking on the path of emancipation, which is the stepping stone towards the freedom of soul. It is the freedom from the bondage of births and deaths.

The complacent life in this universe is *Diksha*.

The prime *dharma* in this world is *Diksha*.

The wonder in this world is *Diksha*.

The potential to expose happiness from the soul is *Diksha dharma*.

So eventually, what is *Diksha*?

In reality, it is the act of stepping out of the householder's life and entering into the company of religious saints and recluses. This act of turning out the worldly garbs and adorning the garbs of unattachment is *Diksha*.

Diksha is the acceptance of 5 sheer pledges:

1. Non-violence or *ahimsa*.

2. Non stealing or *asteya*

3. Non-lying or *asatya*.

4. Chastity or *brahmacharya*.

5. Non-possession or *aparigrah*.

It has three more additional attachments.

All the five pledges must be obtained and obeyed but along with that:

1. Not to be performed by them.
2. No one should be encouraged to perform these evils, they should not tell anyone to perform these evils.
3. Not applaud or show appreciation if someone is performing.

These three folds have three more diversifications:

1. Not to be performed by our own *Maan* or mind, *vachan* and *kaya*.
2. Not to ask anybody to perform by *Maan, vachan* and *kaya*.
3. Not to applaud if anyone is performing by his *Maan, vachan* and *kaya*.

This is the *swaroop* or characteristic of *Diksha*

Renunciation is to forsake temporal relationships with everybody and establish spiritual relations with every soul.

Renunciation means to waive complete social duties and accept complete spiritual duties.

Renunciation means dedication of *Maan, vachan* and *kaya* to *dev guru* and *dharma*.

The resolution to give '*abhay daan*' or assurance of safety to each and every microorganism in present and future till the end of life is true *Diksha*.

Diksha relates to the repentance of the sins of the past unaccountable incarnations of eternal period.

The serene rituals by which these profuse sins of uncountable incarnations are being abdicated from the souls is *Diksha* or renunciation.

INITIATION IN THE *DIKSHA* FOLD

The initiation in the *Diksha dharma* is to cut in a single stroke, all temporal relations and links to the sins and bondages in life. It is to yearn for benefit or auspiciousness of every soul.

It does not favour any relationship; no parentage, no lineage and no relatives. All of them are equally aspiring and auspicious souls.

The literal meaning of *Diksha* comes from the etymology of *Diksha*, which is *dik-sha*.

While *Dik* means *'dana'* to confer, *'Sha* means *'shaya'* to destroy.

Thus *Diksha* means to confer well being, pity and auspiciousness to our souls and at the same time to remove inauspiciousness and all things detrimental for our soul because all these detrimental obstacles hinder the soul from moving towards the path of *moksh* or salvation.

Diksha does not mean only the change of name, the legendary change of garbs or outfits. It does not relate to only a change of home or change of country.

It is purely associated with the change of sentiments, change of rudiments and the fundamental principles of life.

Now, who is fit for *Diksha?* Who are the candidates?

Among all the three worlds, only human beings are competent to take *Diksha*

In the celestial world, *swarg* or heaven, there is only one *samyak darshan dharma*.

The animal inhabitants can take only partial renunciation or *virti dharma*.

The inhabitants of hell can reach only till *samyak darshan* or faith in true religion.

Hence among the 84 lakhs nuclei, only human birth enables us to embark on *Diksha* dharma.

Importance:

The heart of *Diksha:*

Diksha is crest jewel of three worlds and quintessence *tatwa or element* in the three worlds.

With *Diksha,* the relation with each and everyone is cut off except the religious relationships.

Here all relationships are maintained without any partiality or without any inclination of my and yours. It treats everyone as one's own relative.

But how should the relation be? It is the relation of the soul. It is the attachment to the soul and not the physique. Now the media of relationship is not physical but spiritual, related to the upliftment of the soul. A *Diksharthi* worries only about our souls and his own while we worry about his body only.

In this universe, the status, wealth, opulence and sensual pleasures are not to be accumulated but to be condemned as this is the core hub of this human life.

In *jain shastras,* there is a ritual of *varsi daan* that deals with giving alms of all different substances i.e. distributing your wealth while you are on the way to the renunciation grounds. The *daan* may consist of many commodities such as rice, *badam,* cash, commodities etc

Its significance is as follows -

A) It serves on forsaking all attachment for these temporal things.

B) It is a symbol of detachment.

C) It is the realization that this status, applaud, wealth and sensual objects are not for procurement but for relinquishment.

D) It serves as an eye opener for the on lookers or the general public that all these mundane things cannot offer permanent happiness.

This is something higher, something more aspiring.

That's the reason that in spite of having all the worldly pleasures, the *Diksharthi* or the soul deserts these things; partaking his possessions in the world and proceeds; leaving behind a trail of knowledge, thinking and pondering of the real facts behind the *varshi daan*. It can be an inspiration for other aspiring souls to follow the same path.

The magnanimity of *Diksha* -

The importance of *Diksha* is vast and its benefits are umpteen. The scriptures say that if the whole world is made of gold and all this gold is used to cater alms in the seven spheres of *dharma* as per god's command, the consequences of that will still not be equal to 48 minutes of *samaik dharma* or renunciation, so just imagine what will be the affect of life time *samaik* dharma or *Diksha*.

Jain *Diksha* is incomparable with the *Diksha* of other cults or religious paths. Our *shravak* path is itself more valuable than their *dev tatwa*. It is hence worthless to compare with their ascetics.

Jain scriptures hence rightfully recite that the people who do not aspire or pine for *Diksha*, then their *shravak dharma* is not worth a coin because those who do not covet for complete *aradhana,* then their *shravak dharma* or partial *aradhana* is also nil.

Again there is a clause here.

If one is beholding a *Diksha,* and if at that time you applaud and appreciate the *Diksha,* then in this or the next incarnations, you will certainly be able to procure *Diksha*

Diksha is thus a new birth as our true birth in the world is *Diksha.* It is the turning point towards the path of ultimate salvation.

Diksha is accompanied by the tonsure of the hair. It does not relate to just the tonsure of the hair of the recluse or the ascetic. It relates to the tonsure of inner *kashay* or passions. Only if their inner feelings are tonsured, then it results in a bona fide recluse or true *Diksha.*

A rich merchant had four daughters in law namely; *Ujjhita* (one who throws away), *Rakshika* (one who preserves), *Bhogavati* (one who eats) and *Rohini* (one who grows something). He gave each of them five grains of rice with an order to preserve them. *Ujjhita* threw the grains and thought to herself, "there are plenty of rice grains in the larder. I shall give others instead". Bhogavati thinks in the same way and eats the grains. *Rakshika* preserves them in her jewel-casket. But Rohini plants the grains and reaps; she again sows the grains and reaps again until at the end of five years. She has accumulated a large stack of rice.

The merchant returns from his journey and asks for the grain rice to his daughters in law and gave authorities according to their levels of intellect. The first, *Ujjhita,* has been given the authority to discard waste from house. The second, *Bhogavati,* to manage kitchen work. The third, *Rakshika* is given the authority to preserve and escort the jewels and gems of house, and the last one i.e. *Rohini,* is given the authority to manage every domain of house i.e. the overall management of household. These four women, whose names are akin, stand for four types of ascetics.

Those ascetics, who do not keep the five great vows, degrade themselves and are discarded by the *sangha*; those ascetics, who keep the five great vows only with a view to fill their begging bowl and to remain attached to food, etc, disqualify themselves from attaining liberation and earn miseries in succeeding births. Those ascetics, who keep the five great vows and carefully live a worthy renunciation life (*Diksha*) are revered and are worshipped by the *sangha* and they procure *Moksh*. Those ascetics who are not content with pretty well keeping of the five great auspicious vows, but they do propagate the vows, attain liberation.

In the story of the two turtles and a jackal, the first who exposed itself to the danger of the jackal, was killed by it. Similarly, the ascetics who expose themselves to the danger of attachment and aversion, i.e. *raga* and *dwesh,* suffer miseries in the cycle of rebirths. Another turtle remained unhurt in the shell and went to its abode in the water. Similarly, the ascetics who conceal their senses; remain in the shield of restrain; remain unhurt by attachment and aversion; and who settle in their own virtuous nature, they attain liberation.

CHAPTER 21

SHRAVAK AND SHRAVIKA DHARMA

Shravak and *Shravika Dharma*

This is the eternal Truth that "Due to *Dharma* there is happiness and due to *Adharma* there is unhappiness".

The souls who carryout *paap karma* via mind, verbal, and physique, they inevitably suffer angst. The souls who via mind, verbal and physique discard *paap* (sinful acts) and perform religious rites are assured of procuring utmost joy in life. Hence every soul should do an earnest attempt to abjure *paap* and to perform religions rites in their life.

To abjure *paap* acts in our life, *Parama Tarak Tirthankar parmatma* has procured a path of *Virati (vow) Dharma,* which has two folds. First is complete *virati* (*sarvavirati*) and second is partial *virati* (*Anuvratas*).

The path of *virati dharma* is not at all fetter for the soul but is armour for the soul. Hence it is not path of unhappiness or bond for the soul but abjuring of *paap* acts always paves towards sheer happiness. The utter abjure of *paap karma* is only feasible by complying *sarvavirati dharma (diksha).* In the *shasan* of *parama Tarak Tirthankar parmatma,* the status of *sarva - virati dharma* has acme and supreme state. The essence of *diksha dharma* is to procure arrant cheer.

Hence who has penchant for arrant cheer but doesn't have fortitude and strength physique to embark on *diksha dharma*, accede to the *shravak dharma-the* second partial *virati-.Anuvrata dharma*. It complies of twelve partial (*Anuvratas* in their life, means to abjure *paap karma* partially. But who has embarked on *diksha dharma* and utterly abjures *paap karma*, that soul gets liberated from unhappiness and becomes monarch of arrant happiness.

Due to dearth of this understanding, almost all souls have this belief that we will try to give-up *paap karma* and live a pious life. But we will not take pledge in our life. The nub behind this is that our predilection for *paap* is intact. Therefore the souls doesn't accede vow in life and gets bonded with *ashubha karma* which is *aviratikarma*.

The crux behind the bond of *karma* is our inclination or propensity to perform *paap,* which is the root cause for binding of the soul with *karma*. Hence though when *paap* act is not yet performed, the influx of *paap karma* continues. As the propensity to do *paap* is intact, so when the pledge of *paap* acts is being taken, the acts will gradually fade our propensity too.

Hence who has destiny for arrant happiness should at least try gradually to abjure purposeless, inessential, vicious *paap* acts from their life and undertake these 12 *anuvratas* of *shravak dharma* as they are armour for the soul which protects the soul from getting birth as a low-inhabitant.

The sphere of *avartipap karma* is massive, hence for that these twelve *anuvratas* of *shravak* are akin to fence to terminate influx of *asubha paap karma* on soul.

In onset while accepting twelve vows, first in its root there should be acceptance of *samyak darshan* - (Right perception, Right conviction). This is the pedestal for complying twelve vows.

The characteristics of Rights-conviction are.

1. To accept *sadguru* and *saddharma*.
2. To abjure *asadguru* and *asaddharma*.

3. Utmost predilection for *Jinashasan*.

4. To strongly believe in the nine *tatvas*, the cardinal elements of universe.

The path to ascend towards *moksh* has two folds:

First is *Diksha marg*, the Renunciation, full vows. Second is *Shravak* and *Shravika marg*, partial vows. There are twelve vows of *shravaks* and *shravikas*: every layman should adopt these vows according to their capacity and circumstances with the intent to ultimately adopt full vows of renunciation. Then only their partial vows of shravak *dharma* will be fruitful, otherwise it will be in vain. Without adopting any of these vows, they are not *shravak* also. The twelve vows of *shravaks* and *shravikas* are, among which the five main vows of limited nature (*Anuvratas*) means minor vows are:

1. Ahimsa *Anuvrata:* - limited vow of non-violence.

2. *Satya Anuvrata:* - limited vow of truthfulness.

3. *Achautya Anuvrata:* - limited vow of non-stealing.

4. *Brahmacharya Anuvrata:* - limited vow of chastity.

5. *Aparigraha Anuvrata:* - limited vow of possessions.

Three Merit vows (*Guna-vratas*) are:

6. *Disha Vrata:* - vow for limit in movement in any direction.

7. *Bhoga- Upabhog Vrata:* - vow for limited use of consumable and re-consumable things.

8. *Anartha-dandavrata:* - vow for avoidance of purposeless sins.

Four Disciplinary vows (*Shiksha-vratas*) are:

9. *Samayik Vrata:* - vow of equanimity for 48 minutes of duration.

10. *Desawagasika Vrata:* - vow to perform 8 *samayik* and 2 *pratikaman* on *vrataday.*

11. *Paushadha Vrata:* - vow of ascetic's life for one day and over night or only over night.

12. *Atithi Samvibhag Vrata:* - vow of charity.

5 main vows:

Of those twelve vows, the first five are the main vows but small vows or limited vows in comparison with the great vows- *Maha-vratas.*

The *Maha-vratas* are for ascetics.

The next three vows are known as virtue vows (*Guna-vratas*), so called because they enhance and purify the defects of the five main vows and raise their value manifold.

The last four vows are known as disciplinary vows (*Shiksha-vratas*):

These four vows are the matrix (an environment in which something develops) for the souls to develop own self for this supreme vows- *Maha-vratas,* as every soul doesn't have that *saatvicta* that they can directly embark on *Maha-vrata,* the ascetic life. So it enhances the soul to move towards *Maha-vrata* by practicing the *Anu-vrata* i.e. small *vrata.*

Five main vows (*Anuvratas*):

1. Small vow (*Anuvrata*) of non-violence (*Ahimsa Anuvrati*):- In this vow, a person should not intentionally hurt any *Tras* (movable-gross) living-being.

   These are the vows for not doing or abstaining:

   i. I will not do abortion.

   ii. If I have to punish any faulty soul, I will not punish it with cruelty,

iii. I will not grow gardens, plants, trees, lawns, farms, orchards, etc.

iv. I will take care that there should be no sprouting of moss (green fungus) in any place where there is water in the house.

v. On *parvatithi*, I will not grind, wash clothes, clean house, use vegetables and fruits for eating, etc.

vi. I will not take a bath in swimming pools, water parks, lakes, seashore, etc.

vii. I will not use pest control in house for killing insects, etc.

2. Small vow of truthfulness (*Satya Anuvrata*):- In this second vow, big 5 lies are to be ceased:

    i. Do not speak lie for one's own offspring's regarding age, qualities, habits, physical or mental fitness, etc.

    ii. Do not speak lie for one's own animals regarding age, milk, or any other faults of them.

    iii. Do not speak life for one's own land, farm, buildings, office, store, row house or any estate.

    iv. If someone has kept their capitals or opulence at your house for safety, when they come to collect it, do not speak lie that it is not with you.

    v. Do not give wrong evidence by which someone suffers a loss of money, property or goodwill.

3. Small vow of non-stealing (*Achaurya Anuvrata*):- The properties which are not being given by his master can't be taken by us.

    i. I will not do tax stealing.

    ii. I will not travel without tickets.

    iii. I will not do stealing, etc.

4. **Small vow of chastity (*Brahmacharya Anuvrata*):-** To have satisfaction in one's own spouse and abstain from all other opposite sex.

    i. I will follow chastity before marriage.

    ii. I will follow chastity on *parvatithi,* auspicious days, on one's own birthday etc.

    iii. I will follow chastity for some days in a month.

    iv. I will forswear touch of other women.

    v. I will not see blue films, pornography, erotic readings, form and beauty of other women, etc.

    vi. To follow celibacy when on a pilgrimage.

    vii. I will not marry a widow and won't applaud when someone is doing so.

    viii. I will not enjoy unchastity during daytime.

5. **Small vow of non-possession (*Aparigraha Anuvrata*):-** Non-possession is the fifth limited vow.

As long as a person does not know the richness of joy and peace that comes from within, he tries to fill his empty and insecure existence with this clutter of material acquisitions.

One most impose a limit on one's needs, acquisitions and possessions such as land, estate, goods, jewelry, animals, opulence, clothes, vehicles, money, etc. Avarice is the father of all sins. These faults embrace all other passions (*kashay*) in our life. The penchant for possessions is predominant cause for hell.

Three Merit vows:

(6) 1. Limit in area and direction (*Disha Vrata*):- This vow limits one's worldly activities to areas comprising all the ten directions: East, West, North, South, North-east, North-west, South-east, South-west, upward and downward.

   i. I will not travel out of India.

   ii. In monsoon, I will not leave my own place.

   iii. On *parvatithi*, I will not go out of station.

   iv. I will not move in any place for enjoyment.

   v. I will not travel in a plane (upward).

   vi. I will not go under water in submarines for enjoyment and other water amusement parks too (downward).

(7) 2. Vow of limited use of perishable and non-perishable items (*Bhoga-Upbhoga Vrata*):- Perishable (*Bhoga*) objects include those things that can only be used once, such as food and drinks. Non-perishable (*Upbhoga*) objects include those that can be used several times, such as clothes, ornaments, furniture, buildings and women.

In this vow we can take 14 vows daily: the 14 vows of self restraint

The beautiful and life saving vows are called *bhog-upbhog vrat*.

Bhog means the things we use once and *upbhog* means things that we use again and again...

The vows are taken two times...in the morning and in the evening. Because requirements are minimal at night...so why pay for things you are not going to use at all.

The vows are two fold...

They can be restrained by weight and

They can be restrained by figures.

Meaning you vow to take only one kilo of grains per day or you can even restrain saying that you will eat only 40 things per day...

The fourteen vows are:-

1. *Sachit*...Animated substances

2. *Dravya*...Commodities

3. *Viigai*...Aphrodisiac substances

4. *Upaan* or *vanah*....Shoes, chappals etc

5. *Tambol*....Betel, mouth fresheners

6. *Chiror* or *vastra*...Clothes

7. *Kusuma*....Aromatic substances

8. *Vhan*....Vehicles

9. *Ashatana*...Bed, linen etc

10. *Vilepan*...Products to be smeared or applied

11. *Brahmachacharya*....Vow of celibacy, chastity

12. *Disha*.. Directions

13. *Snana*... Bathing

14. *Baktapan*....Food and drinks

Now to know in detail what each vow includes:

1.) Animate substances:-

This includes all living things. Things that can grow again...All living things...raw vegetables.

All flowers, cereals, beans, salt. All these things experience the feeling of touch....they can reproduce again if unused...it is true that we cannot live without using them but we can control the amount we use.

The vow can be thus put as:

i. I won't use animated things for one day.

ii. I will eat only four animated things today and give *abhaydaan* to the rest of the living things on this earth.

iii. I will remove the live portion and use the substance...like removing the seed from the fruit and keeping it aside for 48 minutes so it can thrive again and we can consume the inanimate pulp or skin.

This vow will limit our intake and restrain our mind from indulging in things that we do not consume.

2.) Commodities:-

This refers to the number of eatables that you want to consume throughout the day. From morning to evening, you can decide on how many varieties of food you want. Say thirty or twenty; you can keep a count of it like chapatti, vegetable, salad, pickle etc. Now this does not include the quantity of similar foods. Say you eat four chapattis, so that will be one *dravya* only.

You can also decide on how many drinks you are planning to have

At the end of the day you can sit and contemplate on how many commodities you used. If it is less than what you had decided, it is a gain for you because you could resist your temptations. The vows must be taken as per your capacity and determinations. Many people survive on five items per day too.

3.) Aphrodisiac substances (*Vigai*) -

These are the eatables which, though energy giving, cause lethargy in our lives. They disturb our mind and consequently affect our thoughts too. They are the culprits for bringing *pramad* or laziness in our *Dharma kriya*. Hence we should try and restrict our intake, and if not all, we should try to avoid at least one everyday so we stop becoming a slave to its intake.

Vigai is of two types:

i. *Maha* Vigai

ii. *Vigai*

- *Maha vigai* is of four types and every Jain must abstain from it:

    a) Honey: It is made by killing or hurting bees. So jains can't have it. Secondly it is so sticky that lots of bacteria and living beings thrive on it and consuming it massacres all these living beings. The bacterial reproduces every second.

    b) Liquor: Liquor in any form makes you forget yourself. You are not aware of what you say or do, your senses are numbed. One is not aware of what one does when he is under the influence of liquor, hence seers ask us to refrain from alcoholic drinks.

    c) Butter: Butter is a breeding place of thousands of microorganisms. Jain seers have proved that consuming butter is as sinful as consuming flesh because it thrives as much as flesh.

    d) Meat: Meat pertains to sinful killing of animals and the flesh is a breeding ground of thousands of living creatures. In the blood in the flesh, so many microorganisms multiply. Killing animals with five senses is very sinful.

All the above are *Maha Vigai* which every Jain should refrain from indulging into. All the four *maha vigai* must be renounced for life.

Now coming to the *vigai*, there are six *Vigais* that can be controlled by taking vows in two ways:

i. By refraining from roots and root vegetables.

ii. By refraining from the raw form alone.

What are these six *Vigais*?

These are as follows:

1) Milk 2) Curds 3) Ghee 4) Oil 5) Sugar 6) Fried items

Refraining these from these roots means not taking it in any form.

Say we take milk *vigai*, if we take from root, then we have to abstain from milk and all milk items like tea, curd, coffee, *barfi* etc

But if we take the vow in raw, then only milk consumption is curtailed and we are entitled to all other things prepared from milk, the basic truth underlying the denial of these *vigai* is that these cause sexual arousal. They invigorate the senses, promote our lust, make us indulgent and are detrimental to the upliftment of the soul. Hence it is necessary to curb their intake.

4.) Shoes:-

It refers to the shoes and sandals one wears per day. It is necessary to decide the number of *chappals* we wish to wear per day and thus restrict our usage. Remember, when we go to select a *chappal* at a shoe shop, put on only the ones which you wish to buy. Otherwise each pair you wear will be counted as one pair and your vow will be broken. Do not wear other *chappals* without reason. The moment you put it on your feet, the counting starts.

5.) Nuts and betel:-

There are many types of mouth fresheners. But we do not eat all in one day, so keep only the amount you want to eat and cut off the others by binding vows. You can even select a quantity say 20 grams per day, so you are saved from the sins of all the mouth fresheners prepared in this world. For the sake of 20 grams we keep our mind open and invite sins for no reason at all.

6.) Clothing:-

We may have numerable clothes but we do not wear all of them in one day, so we can restrict our usage to 5 or 6. This includes all the clothes we wear during day and night.

7.) Aromatic substances:-

This includes all the things which have an aroma. It will include perfumes, deodorants etc. We should take a vow as to approximately how much quantity we will use.

8.) Vehicle:-

You may possess a number of vehicles. You have to restrain it by deciding to use only a limited number of vehicles, and if you have to use public vehicles, then you have to include that in your counting too.

9.) Sleeping and seating devices:-

The counting of the number of items you will use will include bed, bed sheets, pillows, chairs, sofas, couch etc, so you can keep the ones you want to use as free and renounce the others. It includes inside the house and outside at places where we intend to visit, so beware because this counting will include garden chairs, benches, public seats also. Hence before counting consider all the possibilities.

10.) Besmear:-

This refers to all things used physically like oil, soap lotions, hair dye, lotions and the like. You can decide the quality in grams or the number of items you intend to use.

11.) Celibacy:-

It is known as *Brahmacharya,* which refers to refraining from any sexual activity by mind, word or action. One can take the vow for the day or the night or both.

12.) Directions:-

This vow decides on the distance which one keeps free to travel in all the four directions. If one knows his fix path, he can bind himself and restrict entry to all other directions, or he can keep a fixed distance on all the four directions say one kilometer or two kilometer on all sides and at night he can restrain on all the sides. This will help him keep his mid off all travel routes and save him from doing *anartha* and being punished for no fault.

13.) Bathing:-

One can decide the number of times one wants to bath during the day as it helps in saving unnecessary wastage of water.

14.) Food stuffs and liquids:-

This vow binds you to the quantity of food you are going to use and the drinks you are going to drink, this is taken in weight i.e. half a kilo or a kilo in the whole day. Liquid is taken is litres and it will include water, buttermilk, juices, soft drinks, etc.

You are thereby saved of all the rest of the quantities of foodstuffs prepared in the world which you are not going to use anyway. If we do not renounce it, then we carry a part of the sin caused in preparing it since you have not restricted it.

This is like the case of an entrance door. If you leave it open, all Tom, Dick and Harry will enter and irritate you, even animals will come and annoy. By closing the door when you do not want to go out, you will restrict the entrance of all. The same with these vows, by restraining, you can control your thoughts and your sins from entering into your system and mainly it will help you keep your mind under control.

Now the vow for six *Kay* living beings:

1.) *Pritvi kay.* It means all worldly bodies, all things that we take from the earth like salt, collyrium, sand, etc. You need to decide how much grams of this type you intend to take.

2.) *Apkay.* Relates to the amount of water you will be using during the day: to cook, to drink, to bath, and to wash etc. You can keep so many buckets as per your need. This will include water for laboratory purposes too.

3.) *Teukay:* This is related to the fire bodies you will use: light, gas, oven, switches, chargers, massagers, hair straighteners, curlers, dryers etc. You can count the items.

4.) *Vayukay:* This will include all the items you are going to use which uses air and wind: swing, fan, cooler, air conditioner, etc. Plan on how many of them you want to use. Once that is decided, you are saved of the innumerable devices present in the world. If you don't take a vow, you will have to partake on all the sins caused by all the harm done to air bodies in the whole world.

5.) *Vanaspatikay:* This is twofold:-

   i. *Pratyek Vanaspatikay.* The number of *pratyek vanaspatikay* you will use i.e. the living beings with one life, like the weight of vegetables.

   ii. *Sadharan vanaspatikay.* Vegetable bodies with a lot of souls.

One has to decide on the count of both. Onions, potatoes, yam have a lot of minute living organisms in their body. That's why Jain religion asks us to abandon the consumption of such foods.

Then three more things which you use everyday must be reflected and limited:

a) *Asi*: Means the instruments you use to chop, kill, deseed, break, etc like knife, nut cracker, sword, scissor, rifle gun, chopper and the like. One must limit his usage by deciding how many of this is he going to use for the day and should abandon the use of the rest of these injurious harmful tools.

b) *Masi:* Means the items used to write. Ink pen, pencil, correctors, sketch pens, colors, crayons etc. One must give a figure as to how many of these stationary items will he use.

c) *Kashi:* This refers to the implements of agriculture, farming which includes hammer, spade, crowbar, hoe etc. One must calculate on how many of them is he going to use and should keep them free and restrict the others.

Now what is the scientific reason behind taking these vows?

The beautiful picture behind this noble act is to bring awareness in your daily activities and restrict your usage. Ultimately we have to leave all these sinful activities. This is a slow and steady practice.

Say you have a lot of money in the bank. If you don't sit and restrict to how much you will use per day, then anyone and everyone will use it. You won't be aware of how much money you have used up, unnecessary waste would occur and money will be used up and you will be in a pitiable condition.

In the same way if we don't keep count of all our sinful acts, they will keep piling up and will empty all our *punya*.

Hence we must contemplate and decide the meagre amount of these activities i.e. without which we cannot survive and control the activities which are not needed for survival. It will save a lot of living beings. Create *Maitri bhav* or friendliness among us and pave the path for our upliftment.

Savour of the Soul

It will help to limit the influx of *paap karma* towards our soul. All these *paap karma* tarnishes the fairness of our soul and are like an eclipse to our human incarnation.

These vows help to stop the unnecessary influx of sins

The tradition of taking these vows is in the morning and evening, because the vows of the morning are not needed at night like foods, etc.

So let us understand and follow these principles and pray for a life bereft of all these sinful activities.

1. To desist the business of 15 *karmadana*.
2. The *abhaksa* (the food which are restrained from eating). The foods which are not apt to eat, those 22 uneatable items are:

    1. Honey.
    2. Butter, cheese.
    3. Wine.
    4. Non-veg.
    5. Root fruits.
    6. A banyan tree's fruits.
    7. A holy tree's fruits.
    8. Ice.
    9. Poison.
    10. Hail i.e. stone pieces of ice.
    11. Wet mud.
    12. To do dinner after sunset.
    13. The fruits which has uncountable seeds.

14. Pickles.

15. Not to eat curd with beans and pulses.

16. The unknown fruits.

17. Frail fruits, in which there is less to eat and more to throw.

18. Brinjal.

19. Bulb roots, tuberous roots.

20. Not to eat the foods whose taste has changed.

3. The bulbous roots which are of 32 types are being told as not eatable in ethics. The 32 tuberous roots are: Only those are given which are well known and used.

   1. Bulbous roots.
   2. Green turmeric.
   3. *Satavari.*
   4. Aloe Vera.
   5. Sweet potato.
   6. Carrot.
   7. Garlic.
   8. Sprout leaf.
   9. Soft hog plum.
   10. Yam.
   11. Onion.
   12. *Palak bhaji.*

13. *Vathula bhaji.*

14. Mushroom.

15. Green ginger.

16. *Muda*-white onions

17. Poppy seeds.

4. I will not take dinner at night i.e. after sunset, partially or on *parvatithi* etc.

5. I will take a vow of *navakarshi,* means I will eat 48 minutes after sunrise.

6. I will drink boiled water daily or on *parvatithi* days.

7. I will forswear honey, butter, wine and non-veg, as they are *Maha-vigai* door to hell.

8. I will relinquish tobacco, *pan*, cigarette, heroin, etc.

9. I will give up eating things which are kept in a refrigerator.

10. I will not eat *sachita* (animate) fruits and vegetables.

11. To play in the limit and if you want new objects, then the old ones should be discarded first so that the figure of limit doesn't extend.

(8) 3. Vow of avoidance of purposeless sins (*Anarthadanda Vrata*):- *Anartha* means to perform sins without crucial reason; *Danda* means punishment, i.e. the soul procuring pains and agonies. *Anarthadanda* means to perform sins without crucial reason and due to that the soul gets punishment. One must not commit unnecessary or purposeless sins or moral offense as defined below:

i. I will relinquish the 7 addictions:

   A. Wine B. Gambling C. Hunting D. Non-veg E. Unchastity with other women F. Stealing G. Unchastity with prostitutes, call girls, etc.

ii. I will not keep pet birds and animals.

iii. I will not see strangulation, wars, wrestling, circus, pornography, TV, radio, etc for amusement.

iv. I will not do a business of weapons, machines, etc.

v. I will not cut trees, won't pluck fruits and flowers from trees and won't affect the lawns and bushes without a genuine reason.

vi. I will not walk on green lawns, fungus, and places where there are green leaves and where grains and beans pervade on the ground.

vii. I will not involve in nuisance talks of women, food items, kingdoms, etc.

viii. I will not see movies, TV, video, blue films, drama, etc. If not able to totally give up then take vows partially.

ix. I will not give *paap* instruments to others, which include grinder, mixture, knife, stick, cutter, plough, hoe, etc.

Four Disciplinary vows (*Shiksha-vratas*):-

(9) 1. Vow of Renunciation for limited duration (*Samayik Vrata*):- This vow consists of sitting down in one place for at least 48 minutes and concentrating one's mind on religious rites like reading, or learning religious books, or doing meditation, or doing *kshyotsarga*. This *samayik* can be repeated several times in a day.

The pledge of 48 minutes make a person realize the importance of a lifelong vow to avoid all sinful acts and is a stepping stone to a life of full renunciation (*Diksha*). The meaning of *samayik* is by giving up affection and aversion (*Raga* and *Dvesha*) and observing equanimity towards all the souls and substances in the universe.

The inclination of equanimity between one's own self and towards all universal souls without partiality between micro and gross, as all soul's original nature is indifferent. It means that what someone does to me that I don't like, the same thing I should not do to others. If I don't like pain, I should not confer pain to others.

Samayik means conferring *abhaydana* to each and every soul in the universe for 48 minutes through mind, speech and body. Not to kill, not to order anyone to kill, nor to applaud for anyone doing it.

(10) 2. *Desavagasika Vrata:* - In *Desavagasika, shravak* and *shravika* has to perform 8 *samayik* and 2 *pratikaman* and have a penance of at least *ekashana* (to eat only one time in a day). In this vow, do 1 *desavagasika* or more in a year, as per your strength.

    i. That day I will renounce the use vehicles.

    ii. I will not use electronic instruments.

    iii. *I will accept brahmacharya*-celibacy.

    iv. I will desist from doing business acts.

(11) 3. Vow of Ascetic's life (*Diksha*) for limited duration (*Paushadha Vrata*):- In this vow it is imperative for a person to live the life of an ascetic for a day, or for a day and an overnight.

During this time, one should retire to a secluded place or a monastery.

    i. Renounce all sinful acts by mind, speech and body.

    ii. Abstain from seeking pleasure from temporal objects of the senses.

iii. One uses this day in spiritual contemplation, does meditation, engages in *swadhyay* (self study), reads and learns scriptures, worships supreme beings like *Arihantas* and *Siddhas* in different shrines, does *bhakti* of *sadguru* in a monastery, does atonement for wrong deeds by confessing it to guru, do's penance *tap, etc.*

iv. Relinquish adornment of physique.

v. Renounce of unchastity (*abrahmacharya*).

vi. Abandon of food: partially or totally.

vii. Giving up every *sansarik* acts.

This vow promotes and nourishes one's spiritual life and provides training (*shiksha* for an ascetic life. It is a net practice for an ascetic life.

(12) 4. *Atithi Samvibhag Vrata:* - *Atithi* means guest, pious personalities; *Samvibhag* means to share equally with them, means to confer to them.

Atithi samvibhag means to confer food, clothes, medicine, water and other objects of one's own possession to monks, nuns, *shravak, shravika* and pious souls for a particular day when the *vrata* is being taken, by welcoming them to your house and by conferring them with great reverence.

One day- before we have to do the fast for whole day i.e. *upavas* and on the next day, we have to do penance of one time eating i.e. *ekashana;* and impart food and water to *sadhu* and *sadhviji bhagwant* and whatever they have taken in alms, that food only has to be taken for consumption in *tap* or *ekashana*.

The vow can be taken for at least once in a year and if possible, do it for more number of times.

Chapter 22

READING - THE STIMULUS FOR THE SOUL

The mentor for the soul

'A beneficial reading is like a garden carried in the mind.'

'Reading is to the mind what exercise is to the body.'

'Reading makes a man complete.'

There are numerous quotes by famous authors about the benefits of reading.

Just as the garden gives away fragrance, reading ethics provides fragrance to the mind, true tenets make the mind conscious as well as healthy and lively, as the saying goes.

A book, like a landscape is a state of consciousness varying with the readers.

Healthy books are considered as the gift to mankind in our culture. A divine status has been given to the books; we respect them. If we unfold the folders of history, we come to know that almost all great men and women were inspired by one or more good books at one or the other point of time in their life.

A good book is the purest essence to the soul. Nowadays, we are on the fast track of life and there is knowledge flowing from various means like the internet, mobiles, and other communication media.

Still, books hold their unique place in developing a cultural society and bring it to a spiritual surface. As the French novelist Bacon has put in, "Some books are to be tasted, others to be swallowed, and few to chewed and digested."

There is no end of knowledge. And books are an umpteen source of knowledge. A good book is a best friend for today and always.

Once we develop the wonderful art of reading, there is nothing in the world that can deter us from doing so. Nothing can prevent us from experiencing and relishing the sweet world of sheer knowledge.

Just as jewels adorn the body and beautify our physique, reading adorns the mind and enlightens the conscious, resulting in the scenic beauty of the soul.

The internet and modern gadgets have brought the world much closer, made it more compact and much smaller. Modern information technology has given us access to a wide range of knowledge with its cost effective and convenient tools but experience proves that no media in the world gives us the bona fide knowledge and pleasure that can be gained by reading scriptures and good books. This is not a mere statement; we too can experience this truth if we start reading books written by our great gurus.

We are living in a mundane world which is full of tensions and full of stress. Books can relax us, de-stress us and can be a source of joy.

We should read to give our soul a chance to luxuriate and to contemplate. This quote alone goes on to show the importance of reading for leading a matured balanced and peaceful life.

Reading has a lot of advantages...

It makes us aware of the various aspects of life.

It enhances perception of the different dimensions of life.

It gives a solace during the ups and downs of life, during the sorrowful days when we feel forlorn, lonely and depressed. It also serves to take the burden off our shoulders.

It can act as a remedy for various ills in life and it can provide solutions to the unsolved issues in life.

It can put us on a right track of wisdom and it can prove to be the best advisor. A best pal may break our trust but a good book will never desert us and never betray us.

We can also imbibe so many values through books.

In the world of nuclear families where grandparents are not present to provide wisdom stories, books can fulfill their job.

Books can give moral boost and imbibe the values that will last for life.

It can also prove as food to nurture our souls.

It helps in dispelling the darkness of doubts and of ignorance, paving way for the true illumination of the soul by making us realize the endless causes of births and deaths, describing the reason for the eternal roaming in the ocean of infinite *sansar*.

Reading kindles and stimulates the souls and it helps us to transcend our doubts, our misconceptions and encourages us to hunt for the truth and search for the true value of life. It helps to understand the nature of the soul, the cause of rebirth and enlightens the path to emancipation.

In the absence of our gurus and our *Tirthankaras*, books are an excellent substitute for us i.e. *Aagams*.

If our *Gandharas* had not written the *Aagams*, we would have never got to know about the great discourses of our *Tirthankaras*. This is the truth for all the authors, all the writers, and all the poets. Their books made them immortal or their arts would-have died with them and the world would never have been richer as regards to knowledge if books would have been absent. The biographies and autobiographies of the great souls have captured all the beautiful moments of their struggle, all their values, all their preaching, all their sacrifices and all their endurances during the freedom struggle. We can enliven each scene; feel each pain in the expression of words as described in their books. This is the magic of books.

In sad moments, in forlorn moments and in loneliness, we can thrive on the gracious company of books. It can bring peace and serenity to our mind and body. As the saying goes:

"Ocean may sometimes cross their boundaries,

Mountain ranges may sometimes shake; the earth may tremble at times,

A thunderbolt may break at firms; a sun may get eclipsed occasionally

A moon may get eclipsed sometimes

But bona fide reading can never be futile

Good reading can never be fruitless."

Books should be used as substitutes to bad company, to bad acquaintances, negative thoughts, depressions, anxiety, fear and many more.

Many a time, anecdotes of wise men, speculations of experts and hard life of sages inspire us towards diligent introspections and can be the cause of unexpected turn to the events, unexpected new path of life.

As Emma Watson beautifully puts it...

"Books are memories in themselves; just like we play a song, picking up a book again can take you back to another place, another world, to another time."

Chapter 23

SAMYAK GYAN- ABSOLUTE KNOWLEDGE MENTOR FOR THE SOUL

Samyak gyan means absolute right knowledge or correct knowledge.

Right knowledge reveals the true nature of reality and describes it as " *Yatharthabodha Samyak* gyan"

Most of our knowledge is sensory based (*Mati*) and based on recorded knowledge developed by our ancestors in the form of books, articles, papers and other medium (*Shruta*). Jain philosophers include the knowledge acquired directly without any medium by removing the *karmic* veil of the soul. This is known as *Samyak* gyan.

Proper knowledge is essential to provide the right guidance to the soul in its journey towards spiritual upliftment. Right knowledge refers to the proper and relevant knowledge of the *tatvas*.

Knowledge is like a beautiful garden; the more you put into it, the more it grows. The fragrance of flowers pervades in the direction of the wind, but the fragrance of the factual knowledge pervades in all directions. Knowledge or *gyan* is the inherent quality of the soul. It is that characteristic quality of the soul or *atma* that distinguishes itself from *jadh* matter. It is that powerful weapon which has the power to grant cheerfulness, happiness, and gaiety to the soul. It is like a magic wand to vanquish all sadness, sorrow and suffering of this mundane world. It is that wishing stick that can give us freedom from the bondage of birth and death and from eternal pain. Thus it is very necessary to make it our ultimate goal, our destiny, and to arm ourselves with factual knowledge, absolute knowledge, and pious knowledge or in short, *Samyak* gyan.

We should remember that knowledge is like a ship to cross the vast ocean of births and deaths, and of our very existence. It is the light to dispel the darkness of our souls, the darkness of ignorance and the darkness of incorrect vision.

Knowledge can be broadly classified into two categories:

1. Knowledge that cannot bring any change in our life- that cannot transform our life and cannot lead us towards spiritual upliftment.
2. Knowledge that has the potential to change our life -That gives us the power to ascertain right and the wrong, to gauge the beneficial from the harmful, to caution us from the ill treatment of the soul and guide us to the spiritual elevation.

Knowledge that is acted upon becomes wisdom.

Unimplemented knowledge becomes a burden. It is like a donkey carrying the load of sandalwood logs. For the donkey; it is just a burden to carry. He neither realizes the logs worth nor does it appreciate its fragrance.

Whenever we receive any knowledge, we need to pass it through the following tests -

1. Is this knowledge capable of transforming us?
2. Will it help in rubbing out our wrong convictions?
3. Is it beneficial for our soul's upliftment?
4. Will it help us in the path of spiritual fulfillment?
5. Will it take us towards our ultimate goal?

6. Is its truth universally acceptable?

7. Will it carry us on the path of virtuousness and piety?

If the answer is a 'yes', then we further need to analyze the following-

1. Do we believe in it? Do we have faith in it?

2. Can we incorporate it into our lives?

3. Will its incorporation enlighten our lives?

4. Will it take us a scale higher than where we are?

5. Will it deepen our perception?

6. Will our vision be cleared?

7. Will our ignorance be dispelled?

8. Will we shine in the new light of wisdom?

It is only action that translates information. The first and foremost test of knowledge should be the fact that it should be able to transform oneself towards virtuousness and purity or piousness. Knowledge is an ocean of awareness but how true is the knowledge which we have received?

The answer to it is that the higher our knowledge, the higher will be our awareness and maturity. Our perception and insight will be deeper and the same wisdom will take a new shape, pave paths, and unfold more and more meaning and vision for us.

Bona fide knowledge is like a garden. Just as a garden is enriched with innumerable flowers of varied fragrances, colors, hues, sizes and charm; the beauty of which delights and beholds the eyes and the mind of the beholder.

Similarly, the garden of knowledge imparts the beautiful flowers of virtues of varied variety like gratitude, composure, compassion, tranquility and equality; all of which delights the souls that bask in and visit the garden. All these manifold beauties are cherished by the soul.

Knowledge in Action -

Right knowledge manifests into right tenets, and right tenets into right conduct known as *Samyak gyan, Samyak darshan* and *Samyak charitra.* The first stepping stone is a good thought. The second step is a good word and the third step is a good deed. All these are the outcomes of true knowledge. It is like landing in paradise.

The Value & Importance of Knowledge -

1. Knowledge & education are sharp and sacred weapons that help us unshackle our karmas. They aid us in combating the battle of life.

2. It is an instrument to shape our present self and aid in reshaping and reframing our future incarnations in a more beneficial and advantageous way.

3. Knowledge is a treasure that no one can steal. No person, no event, no consequence, good or bad, can be affected by our *paap* or evil virtues.

4. One great quality of this knowledge is that it intensifies and multiplies when we confer it to others and after acquiring it, it has the quality of multiplying profusely and remains in surplus, increasing when imported or exported.

5. Life is not a bed of roses. There are ups and downs. What one sows, one reaps, but acquired knowledge helps us to deal with adverse situations maturely. It helps us to sail in rough weather without losing hope and making matters worse. It makes us to move on tough and difficult paths without losing our sanity or composure.

6. We always get what we crave for. But the yearning must be earnest, sincere and clear. Once this happens, nothing can stop or deter us from reaching our aspirations. Intensity in craving is necessary to attain true knowledge. It must be so incessant that it enables us to cross all hurdles that come in the way of its attainment.

7. Dissatisfaction is the path to greatness. If you are dissatisfied with what you have, you will hunt for greener pastures. Dissatisfaction is the road to real knowledge. It is a true jewel of human birth.

8. Knowledge is a wanting to cross the desperate *sansar*.

9. Growth is a means of maximizing one's potential. The growth can be inner or outer. True knowledge helps one soar internally. The inner growth paves way towards eternal knowledge or *Samyak* gyan. It helps it reaching the full stage of emancipation.

10. Inner personal and spiritual growth can be accentuated with the dissatisfaction of the present state of affairs, and can scale us upwards.

11. When we mould ourselves with true knowledge, then the words which come out are from the depth of truth.

12. With the presence of true knowledge, we are able to perceive a clear stream of reason. We will not be lost in the dreary desert of bad habits. The presence of knowledge has the potential to purge and purify the soul from the filth of vices.

13. The effect of knowledge is a mind without fear and a head held high.

14. True knowledge is not filling a pail of knowledge but igniting a fire of knowledge.

15. Education can serve as a means to improve our persona.

16. True knowledge is judged by a man's intention and his strength of character.

17. The test of knowledge is through composure. If it does not impart composure to other souls then it is just like a parrot repeating words. It is like a library at the tip of the tongue with no changes in the interior.

18. The test of true knowledge is to sacrifice all the things that you and cherish, all of which may or may not be beneficial, but still manage to live happily and blissfully.

19. True knowledge is transcendence. It is the ability to go higher without getting disturbed. It is the maturity gained by true knowledge to climb on the mirth and merry state of the soul whatever be the circumstances.

20. If we develop a capacity to remain deep rooted in our faith however intense the effect of *karma* may be; the true credit goes to knowledge.

21. Education yields humility, humility yields character and character gives us happiness.

22. People will respect you for your education, knowledge, wisdom and maturity. All these are the qualities of the inner self. You will not be measured on the basis of your opulence, wealth and possessions.

23. Education can harvest wealth but wealth cannot harvest education.

24. True knowledge gives the smartness to transcend our weaknesses by not getting transfixed with them.

25. Our mother gives us birth only once but true knowledge can give us birth again and again. With every new initiative we take to change ourselves spiritually, a new person emerges and we discover our new self.

26. True knowledge is to relentlessly strive towards the perfection of spirit.

27. Once we get into the vicious cycle of defending our weaknesses and arguing in favour of them, we become enslaved in its claws. No one can help us out, but knowledge and maturity helps us to recognize our demerits and weaknesses, and encourages us to get free from its clutches.

28. True knowledge makes us realize the reality of life. It probes us to make the best of what we have been bestowed with. Life is an overall package, a few intelligent experiences and a few intruding ones too but we need to start cherishing every package as it is our own past. We should remember that with each package, our soul is getting relieved of bondage of its past *karma*. Let us help in relieving it and not burden it with more sordid *karma*.

29. When you have the ability to listen to almost anything without losing your temper and self confidence, you are truly educated.

Atomic energy is a potential. It can be used as a great creative source or the most destructive one. Similarly, knowledge, power, position, popularity and prosperity are potent forces. They can create everything or destroy everything. It depends on how the potential is directed. If it is intelligently targeted, then it can create wonders.

It is not intelligence but the direction of the intelligence that determines the path of our spiritual growth. It is not necessary that all spiritual people are intelligent. It is the fact that they have given a bona fide direction to their intelligence i.e. *Samyak* knowledge and *Samyak* perception.

True knowledge is a bottomless pit. The higher the maturity, the deeper will be the understanding. The higher I grow in maturity; the same piece of wisdom that I thought I have always understood, will unfold deeper and deeper meanings to me. It will open new doors of understanding for me.

When the soul is watered with understanding, it is endowed with queer shaded flowers and the fragrance of happiness and blissfulness.

After enjoying a gala celebration in the royal retreat of education, one can enjoy the savoury, palatable, colourful and appealing dishes of morals, maturity and *moksh* - all of which help to quench the hunger of happiness.

At the end, there is a sweet desert of the resolution to procure *Samyak gyan* to uplift the soul.'

Once one has tasted this royal treat of education, then he will forever cherish the dishes of values, virtues and vivacity.

GLOSSARY

1. Abated- Fade
2. Abdication- Give up
3. Abide- Accept or act in accordance with
4. Abjure- Give up
5. Abstergent- Purify
6. Abysmal- Very bad
7. Accolade- Praise
8. Acme- Highest point of achievement
9. Acquaintance- Knowledge
10. Adornment- Decorate
11. Affliction- Cause suffering
12. Aftermath- Result
13. Agony- Pain
14. Ail- Ills
15. Akin- Similar
16. Alchemy- Changing a metal into gold
17. Allied- Working together

18. Alms- To give
19. Altruistic- Unselfish
20. Amorous- Sexual desire
21. Armor- Protective metallic covering
22. Analogous- A partial likeness
23. Analogy- Similar
24. Analytical- Logical
25. Anecdotes- Stories about real incidents or persons
26. Angst- Severe anxiety
27. Anguish- Pain
28. Animate- Living being
29. Annihilate- Destroy completely
30. Aplomb- Self possession
31. Appalling- Horrify
32. Applaud- Express approval
33. Apt- Appropriate
34. Archer- Bow
35. Ardent- Passionate
36. Arduous- Difficult
37. Arrant- Complete
38. Articulate- To express
39. Aspirant- Hopeful
40. Asrava- Influx of *karma*

41. Assuage- Soothe
42. Astound- To amaze
43. Atheist- Person not believing in god
44. Atonement- Make amend for a fault
45. Attribute- Characteristic quality
46. Autonomy- Opposite
47. Avail- Benefit
48. Avarice- Greed
49. Averment- Law to prove or justify
50. Awful- Extremely bad
51. Axiom- An accepted principle
52. Barren- Fruitless
53. Beatitude- Happiness
54. Begets- Arouse
55. Besmear- Cover with something
56. Bestow- Give
57. Betrayed- Disloyal
58. Black lash- Result
59. Bona fide- Genuine
60. Boons- Benefit
61. Candor- Frankness
62. Captivation- Attract
63. Caste- Throw

64. Cater- To give
65. Celestial- Heavenly
66. Celibacy- Abstaining from marriage, etc
67. *Chaira*-Restrain
68. Chiseling- Process of curving stone with a sharp tool.
69. Compassion- Pity
70. Complacent- Self satisfied
71. Composure- Calmness
72. Comprehend- Understand
73. Conceit- Ego
74. Condemned- Express disapproval
75. Confound- Confuse and Surprise
76. Conscientious- Diligent in your duty
77. Consistent- Continuous
78. Contemplate- Think deeply
79. Copulation- Sexual relation
80. Corrode- To east away, rust
81. Covet- Desire
82. Crucial- Very important
83. Crucify- Put to death
84. Crux- Key point
85. Deceit- Proud
86. Decipher- Understanding or interpreting something

87. Decorum- Correctness
88. Defilement- Dirty
89. Delude- Mislead
90. Deemed- Regard something in a specified way
91. Denial- Refusal
92. Depurate- To pure
93. Desperate- Intense desire
94. Detrimental- Tending to cause harm
95. Devastate- Ruin
96. Deviation- Diverge
97. Device- Tool
98. Dilemma- Problem
99. Dire- Horrible
100. Disastrous- Causing great damage
101. Discourse- Sermon
102. Dispel- Drive or Clear away
103. Disport- Different
104. Dogma- Fixed Opinion
105. Domination- Have commanding influence
106. Dough- Money
107. Dreadful- Horrible
108. Dwell- Think About
109. Ecstasy- Happiness

110. Ecstatic- Happiness
111. Elaborate- To explain in detail.
112. Élan- Energy and Flair
113. Elation- Happiness
114. Elucidate- Explain
115. Emancipation- Salvation
116. Endeavour- Earnest attempt
117. Endorsement- Favor
118. Endow- Give
119. Engender- Give rise to
120. Enigma- Mysterious thing
121. Enshrine- Respect
122. Entice- Attract by offering pleasures
123. Ephemeral- Transient
124. Erudite- Learned
125. Eternal- Everlasting
126. Eunuch- Castrated Man
127. Euphoria- Exited happiness
128. Evade- Escape or Avoid
129. Existential- Be present somewhere
130. Expound- Explain
131. Exuberant- Happiness
132. Fabulous- Extraordinarily great

133. Fake- Pretend
134. Fascination- Intense attraction
135. Fathomless- Endless
136. Feasible- Possible
137. Felicity- Happiness
138. Ferment-Excitement
139. Fervor- Passion, Zeal
140. Fetters- shackle
141. Flow- Fault
142. Forlorn- Pain
143. Forlorn- Unhappy
144. Fortitude- Strength of mind
145. Forum- Place
146. Foul- Very bad
147. Fringe- Outer patrol area
148. Frugally- Prudently
149. Futile- Fruitless
150. Gaiety- Happiness
151. Genealogy- History of families from generation to generation
152. Gist- Essence
153. Glee- Happiness
154. Goad- To guide
155. Halt- Stop

156. Hanker- Crave
157. Haywire- Out of control
158. Hearth- Fire place
159. Hurling- Throwing with force
160. Hub- Core
161. Hues- Color
162. Ignited- Kindle
163. Illumination- To light up
164. Illusion- Misconception
165. Impasse- A deadlock
166. Imbibe- To absorb ideas
167. Immaculate- Clean, Pure
168. Imprecise- Not precise
169. Incarnation- Birth
170. Inclination- A natural tendency to act in a particular way
171. Indignations- Anger because of wrong done, especially to yourself
172. Indolence- Laziness
173. Infatuated- enamored
174. Influx- Incoming
175. Inferno- Hell
176. Inhabitants- Person
177. Innate- Inborn, Natural

178. Instigate- Provoke
179. Interlude- A thing occurring during an interval
180. Intrigued- Curiosity
181. Jeopardize- To put in danger
182. *Kadai-* Type of a vessel
183. Kindred- Family, Relatives
184. Leisure- Free time
185. Leverage- Power
186. Lewdness- Sexual matter
187. Lucid- Clear
188. Lure- Attract
189. Lust- Intense sexual desire
190. Macabre- Horrible
191. Magnanimous- Noble and Gentle
192. Mainspring- Reason
193. Manifestation- Phase
194. Melancholy- Great sadness
195. Metaphor- Similitude
196. metaphysically- Religious knowledge
197. Metaphysics- Spiritual knowledge
198. *Mithyatva-* Wrong belief
199. Mortal- Subject to death
200. Mull- Think over

201. Mundane- World
202. Muse- Think over
203. Nefarious- Evil act
204. Negate- Deny the existence
205. *Nirajar*- Detachment of *karma*
206. Nubile- Sexually mature
207. Nurture- Care for
208. Onerous- Difficult
209. Onset- Beginning
210. Ousts- To expel from position or place
211. *Padarth*- Substance
212. Panacea- Remedy for all diseases
213. Paradox- Self contradictory
214. Paramount- Chief
215. Parenthesis- Brackets
216. Passion- Excitement
217. Passionate- Intense
218. Penance- *Tap*
219. Penchant- Strong liking
220. Perceptible- Becoming aware or conscious of
221. Perpetual- Never ending
222. Perturb- Disturbs
223. Pervade- Spread

224. Philanthropy- The habit of helping people
225. Pierce- Hole
226. Pinnacle- High point
227. Pledge- Vows
228. Plinth- Base
229. Polygamy- Having more than one or more wife or husband
230. Ponder- Deep thinking
231. Potential- Ability, Capacity
232. Preceptor- Guru
233. Predilection- Strong liking
234. Pristine- Original
235. Proclivity- Inclination
236. Procure- Gain
237. Profuse- Plentiful
238. Propensity- Tendency
239. Propitious- Auspicious
240. Provoke- Arouse
241. Prowess- Skill
242. Prudent- Wise
243. Prurient- Given to unclean thought
244. *Punya*- Auspicious *karma*
245. Purport- To mean
246. Queer- Unusual

247. Quiddity- Bring back to life
248. Quintessence- Heart
249. Rage- Violent, Anger
250. Rapture- Intense delight
251. Reign- Rule
252. Refrain- Keep hold
253. Relinquish- Give up
254. Relish- Great enjoyment
255. Renounce- Give up
256. Renunciation- Give up
257. Repugnant- Extremely bad
258. Resentment- Dislike, Grudge
259. Resurrect- Bring back to life
260. Retrospect- Looking back on a past event
261. Reverence- Deep respect
262. Rites- Religious acts
263. Romp- Live play
264. Ruminate- Think deeply
265. Ruthless- Pity full
266. Sabotage- Destroy
267. *Sadhu-* Monk
268. *Sadhvi-* Nuns
269. Salubrious- Health giving

270. *Samyak darshan*- Right belief
271. Savant- Learned man
272. Savour- Taste
273. Scenario- Events
274. Scenic- Relating to beautiful natural scenery
275. Serene- Calm and Peaceful
276. Sheer- Pure
277. *Shravak*- Laymen
278. *Shravika*- Laywomen
279. Slander- Malicious gossip
280. Slime- Dirt
281. Sloping- Bend, Forward
282. Smolder- Fire without smoke
283. Smudge- Dirty
284. *Sadhana*- Rituals
285. Soar- To rise
286. Sonorous- Rich, Deep
287. Sordid- Dirty
288. Spectacular- Impressive
289. Spur- Encourage
290. Spurn- Reject
291. Squalid- Extremely dirty and unpleasant
292. Stacking- Keeping

293. Staunch- Very loyal
294. Strenuous- Difficult
295. Sturdy- Strong
296. Stubble- Micro
297. Stupendous- Amazingly good
298. Stupor- Dazed condition
299. Sublimation- Purifying
300. Sublime- Highest excellence or Beauty
301. Substantiate- Support with evidence
302. Succession- Sequence
303. Surveillance- A close watch
304. Tabooed- Prohibited
305. Tenets- Belief
306. Theist- Person believing in god
307. *Tirthankar-* God
308. Toils- Work hard
309. Tough- Strong
310. Tranquility- Peace or Calm
311. Transcend- Exceed, Surpass
312. Transverse- Cross wise
313. Treacherous- Unreliable, dangerous
314. Trigger-Activates
315. Turbulence- Disorder

316. Turmoil- Confusion
317. Ubiquitous- Found everywhere
318. Umpteen- Indefinitely many
319. Validate- Valid, Legalize
320. Venomous- Poisonous
321. Vile- Evil
322. Virgin- Person who never had sex
323. Virtual- Reality
324. Vitality- Power
325. Vivacity- Happiness
326. Vivid- Clear, Bright, Lively
327. Waive- Give up
328. Wiles- Tricks
329. Whirlpool- Current of water in a circle
330. Yearn- Crave
331. Yell- Cry
332. Yen- Crave
333. Zeal- Enthusiasm
334. Zenith- Highest

www.ingramcontent.com/pod-product-compliance
Lightning Source LLC
Chambersburg PA
CBHW031347040426
42444CB00005B/219